ROOTED

Rooted

An Introduction to Christian Theology

LAURA HEWETT

Laura Hewett

Copyright © 2021 by Laura Hewett

All rights reserved. No portion of this book may be reproduced in any manner whatsoever without written permission except in the case of brief quotations embodied in critical articles and reviews.

To request permissions of use, contact the author at sainthewett@gmail.com.

First Printing, 2021

Illustrations by: Leah Finke
Cover art by: Givorgy Kraskoff

www.sainthewett.com

Contents

Introduction vi
The Apostles Creed ix

ONE
THE TRINITY THEOLOGY PROPER

TWO
JESUS | CHRISTOLOGY

THREE
THE HOLY SPIRIT PNEUMATOLOGY

FOUR
THE CHURCH ECCLESIOLOGY

FIVE
PEOPLE ANTHROPOLOGY

SIX
SIN & SALVATION HAMARTIOLOGY & SOTERIOLOGY

SEVEN
END TIMES ESCHATOLOGY

EIGHT
THE BIBLE BIBLIOLOGY

Selected Bibliography 85
Acknowledgements 87

Introduction

After teaching a Bible course to teenagers at a private high school for several years, I struggled to get students to engage with the textbook I was using. It's a great book on it's own, but it wasn't written for young people to read and learn about the Christian faith in a classroom setting. This book you are now reading is my attempt to write a high school level text that engages the students in my classroom with the complementing curriculum. Its chapters are based on the ten doctrines I cover in the second unit of my course. They are written to give a broad ecumenical overview of the topics. I need this because I teach students from so many denominational backgrounds, and I want to encourage critical thinking and compassion for views from a wide range of perspectives - particularly within Christianity.

My hope is that my students and other readers will encounter in this text an affirmation of what Christians broadly hold to be true while acknowledging the beauty in different nuanced positions within the broad catholic of the church. Because this is written as an overview of so many denominations and theological positions, I make no attempt to elucidate all the detailed minutiae of most issues. Instead, my goal is to give readers an understanding of the core or essential doctrines of the Christian faith and introduce them to the variety of perspectives held within orthodox communities. Because this is meant to teach about Christian beliefs, I do use theological terms and situate them within church history, but I have done my best to use accessible language rather than sticking in the fancy pants seminary terms or ancient theologians without explanation.

I chose to organise the chapters according to content in the Apostles' Creed because while there are so many systematic theologies that cover a variety of doctrines, I wanted to anchor my text in the broad strokes of what all Christians agree on through church history. By the grace of God, it is not my responsibility to determine the salvation of others, and I dare not have the audacity to add or detract from what church leaders beginning over fifteen centuries ago agreed to call essential in the Christian faith, so I stay anchored to this ancient affirmation in explaining what all Christians believe. Each chapter except the last begins with a quote or passage of the creed, and then I begin by introducing the theological term and what is covered in the chapter. The final chapter I included is on the Bible because that is the sacred text of Christianity that Jesus followers look to for development of theological perspectives as well as personal growth. I tried to respect terms and definitions that are commonly used today while addressing the evolving understanding and application thereof.

One unique feature of this text is that throughout the whole book, I avoid using biblical prooftexts when describing each doctrine affirmed by the whole church. I absolutely believe there is biblical affirmation of each of these, but I have a couple reasons for avoiding the common practice of citing verses to back up claims. First, this is written as a textbook for high school students, and the parenthetical citations are frequently glazed over by Christian teenagers who have heard John 3:16 a million times and heard countless other verses whipped out as weapons in verbal battles of interpretive nuances. My course and therefore this book are meant to open discussions rather than shut down conversations as prooftexts are often used to do.

Additionally, prooftexts are often an interpretation of a phrase or short passage that don't consider the context, and because my goal is to provide a wide overview of ecumenical positions, prooftexts will derail from a clear presentation of the consensus among Christians based on a wide reading of biblical texts and Christian practices. Instead, I've put footnotes with Scripture references to several points where there's a large consensus of interpretation.

As the adage attributed to Athanasius[1] goes, let us have, "in essentials unity, in nonessentials diversity, and in all things charity."

[1] Though Rupert Meldenius actually deserves more credit for coining the phrase.

The Apostles Creed

*I believe in God, the Father Almighty,
Creator of Heaven and earth and in Jesus Christ,
His only Son Our Lord,
Who was conceived by the Holy Spirit,
born of the Virgin Mary,
suffered under Pontius Pilate,
was crucified, died, and was buried.
He descended into Hell;
the third day He rose again from the dead;
He ascended into Heaven,
and sits at the right hand of God,
the Father almighty; from thence
He shall come to judge the living and the dead.
I believe in the Holy Spirit,
the holy catholic Church,
the communion of saints,
the forgiveness of sins,
the resurrection of the body and life everlasting.*

ONE

The Trinity
Theology Proper

I believe in God, the Father Almighty, Creator of Heaven and earth

Christianity is one of the world's major monotheistic religions. We believe in one God. We use unique language to describe our one God, however: Father, Son, and Holy Spirit. In Christian churches, we refer to this as the Trinity. The word "trinity" is never used in the Bible, but the concept is critical enough that early church leaders made a point to use trinitarian language in their doctrine statements and letters. Fancy pants theologians and regular readers alike find reference to the concept throughout the whole Christian Bible. While it is a central and emphasised doctrine within Christianity, every Christian will readily admit that the Trinity is a difficult concept to comprehend. It bends beyond what humans easily grasp, and every analogy to explain it will fall short. That, however, shouldn't stop us from pursuing a basic understanding of the concept. This chapter provides an overview of how early church leaders described God and came to value clear thinking about the Trinity while avoiding misrepresentations. Tracing that history of affirmations and disagreements helps us to have greater confidence and understanding in our beliefs.

The Apostles' Creed[1] begins by identifying the three members of the Trinity and giving the attribute "Creator of Heaven and earth" to the Father. In fancy theological terms, we say *theology proper* when talking about the study of God the Father specifically, but Christians often blur that one member of the Trinity as the one that is plain "God" while having more distinctions in their mind for the other two. When thinking of God in the Christian worldview, it's important to keep all three members of the Trinity in mind as fully God. Unfortunately, some people slide into describing the Trinity as God, Jesus, and the Holy Spirit which leads to complicated and incorrect ideas about the Father being more important.

This equal status of the three members was so important to early church leaders, however, that the Eastern Orthodox church made an official split with the Western church when leaders in the West updated the creed to include the idea of "procession" when talking about the relationship of the Spirit to the Son and Father. This wasn't just some agree-to-disagree opinion like what kind of hat priests should wear (though you can distinguish leaders of various church traditions today by their distinct headgear). Those siding with the Eastern Orthodox church over this doctrinal statement claimed that the updated language makes it seem like the Holy Spirit is a subordinate member of the Trinity or a later existing one. The language of the Nicene Creed[2] carefully says the Son is "begotten not made" to indicate the special Father/Son relationship Jesus has within the Godhead as one who is also eternally existing as fully God. That wasn't sufficient to satisfy the Eastern leaders, but we'll look at that split more in our chapter on the church. Keep in mind for now that all Christians affirm the equality of each member of the Trinity.

Different denominations have developed language around their understanding of the relationship between the members of the Trinity, though, and two broad categories are the vertical and horizontal ordering. In the vertical or *hierarchical* understanding of the Trinity, Christians are comfortable with the language of procession and begotten because they affirm that while all members of the Trinity are coequal in power, they have a hierarchical order in their relationship. You may hear your teachers or pastors who hold this position describe how the Father makes plans, the Son enacts, and the Spirit oversees. They read texts like Jesus' praying in the Garden of Gethsemane "not my will but yours be done"[3] as an example of submission to the will of the Father, and further examples of Jesus telling his disciples that he will send the Holy Spirit as a helper to them when he leaves[4] are interpreted as yet another organisational feature of the Trinity. "God is not a God of disorder, but of peace,"[5] these theologians eagerly affirm. Their religious art will often show God the Father sitting on a great throne as a large figure with a smaller man on his lap (adult or baby features differ but the size of God the Son is of significance) and God the Holy Spirit as a dove alighting somewhere near Jesus.

In response to the hierarchical position, other theologians prefer seeing the icons of three equally sized humanlike images though often with different items or clothing to differentiate between members of the Trinity. This could be described as a *horizontal* understanding of the Trinity. Most famous among the visual representations of this position is Rublev's icon of the Trinity from the fifteenth century. In this famous painting, three angels are depicted as human looking representations of the Father, Son, and Holy Spirit. Behind each of them is a different item that theologians associate with concepts of the different person's actions or engagement in the world - a house, a tree, and a mountain. The persons incline their heads towards each other and share the sacrifice presented before them equally. The position of the angels representing the members of the Trinity is also intentional to create a circle showing the unity among them. Theologians siding with this horizontal understanding of the Trinity emphasise instructions from Jesus at the end of Matthew that commissions all Christians to make disciples and baptise in the name of the Father, the Son, and the Holy Spirit with no distinction of rank.[6] These complicated fights within the early church show the significance of representing the truth about the Trinitarian God accurately.

Common Mistakes to Avoid

The following examples from early Christian thinkers show how leaders in the church wanted to make sure they explained the Trinity carefully and clearly rebuked *heresy* (the technical word for ideas outside the bounds of Christianity or, more simply stated, a *heresy* is a non Christian idea). Looking at how previous Christians either provided good examples or instead overstepped in their analogies can help us to have healthy boundaries in our understanding of God. Learning from church history shouldn't put blinders to any truth but rather be lampposts to keep us from veering off into bad theology. Just like we want to avoid thinking of the Father as the only "God" part of the Trinity and subordinating the Son and Holy Spirit in our conversations and thoughts, we can learn some helpful boundaries by looking at the limits of analogies.

For example, Saint Patrick, a fifth century pirate slave turned missionary to Ireland, is famously credited with explaining the Trinity as one God in three parts like the single clover has three leaves. This, taken to its extreme, however, results in the heresy of *partialism* - the idea that the one God has three separate parts that operate and exist independently. The interdependence and unity of the Trinity is consistent in descriptions of different members of the Trinity within the Bible. Other common trinitarian heresies include *modalism* or *Sabellianism* - the ideas that God either operates as different members of the Trinity at different times or just manifests in different forms for different purposes. *Arianism* and others like it believe that either Jesus was a lesser level deity or somehow the Son and Spirit are lower ranking gods to the Almighty Father.

With some good examples of the extremes we want to avoid when thinking about the Trinity, church leaders worked to develop a simple positive description of God within the Christian worldview. The Athanasian Creed[7] spends a large portion of the text emphasising the equal and distinct nature of the persons of the Trinity. The primary claim reads, "we worship one God in Trinity, and Trinity in Unity; neither confounding the Persons, nor dividing the Essence." This struggle to understand the Trinity comes from the fact that created, mortal humans have a limited capacity to understand an uncreated, eternal God. Many heresies began as honest attempts to understand the Divine. Analogies can be helpful, but it's critical to remember that any analogy taken to its extreme will lead to heresy. Paul E. Little puts it perhaps in the most succinct way to remember: "God *is* one being, but he exists in three persons."[8]

While unsatisfying to some that we cannot understand the details of how the Trinity operates, perhaps a better perspective within the Christian church is that our God is sufficiently more complex than we are and therefore worthy of the worship we choose to give. At this point in lessons, I often have students throw up their hands and say, "If I can't understand the mystery of the Trinity perfectly, why even bother learning anything at all about God?" My response is an emphatic celebration that God is *infinitely knowable*. The God of the Bible has chosen to reveal plenty of consistent, unchanging, and *personal* characteristics.

God's Character

There are volumes filled with theologians expounding on the character of God, so here in this chapter, I'll just give a few definitions of features the Bible affirms about who God is and how God acts. An important note on God's character is that Christians believe in a consistent God. As the Bible was written and God interacted with humans, the human understanding of God grew, but God's character remained consistent. Tim Mackie and his team at The Bible Project begin their explanation of God by visualising how those in a 2D plane struggle to make sense of a 3D object interacting with it. Similarly, humans have different descriptions of God through the Bible that give us a fuller picture of who God is which sometimes require deeper thought and consideration.

Three of the first words most frequently used to describe God are the "omni" words which use the Latin root *omni* (which means *all*) to describe the fullness of God's abilities. *Omnipotent* is a description of God's strength and ability to do anything; God is all powerful. Christians recognise this to mean that God can do great feats of strength as well as miracles. This is described frequently in the Bible as God parts great waters, shuts the mouths of lions, stops the rain, multiplies food for the hungry, heals the paralysed, and even raises people from the dead. *Omniscient* refers to God's intelligence; God is all knowing. There are examples of this when God tells humans what other people are planning (like Elisha knowing the plans of the Syrian king[9]) or when Jesus calls out the Pharisees about what they are thinking.[10] Here there is some complicated disagreement among Christians as many theologians believe God knows what can happen and therefore sees many futures that could play out dependent upon human choices while other theologians emphasise God's knowledge of all the choices that will be made leads to God knowing the exact future always. What Christians do agree on is God's omniscience is a supreme knowledge above human knowledge or that of other spiritual beings. *Omnipresent* is a reference to God's lack of temporal restrictions; God is present in all places. This doesn't mean that God *is* all things but rather that God's presence is *in* all places. For example, God is not a tree, but God is present when you walk into a forest.

God's *sovereignty* is another feature Christians generally agree relates to God being in charge of the world. The critical nuance of this attribute among theologians is connected to theodicy, the study of suffering. That argument extends far beyond the reach of this book, but it is important to touch on the tension that Christians have in affirming God as both all powerful (omnipotent) and in charge of the world (sovereign) when bad things happen to good people. The simplest response is that God allowed and valued free will in creation which led to brokenness, suffering, and hurt. What is most important to recognise in this feature of God's character is that the sovereignty of God ought never to lead us into believing that God inflicts the suffering and hurt in the world. Greg Boyd in his book on theodicy gives a helpful analogy to how we can view God like a king in charge but not inflicting suffering even when his delegates don't do what he wants because in some sense the delegates are an extension of the king himself. Boyd says, "In this sense, everything humans and angels do is seen as coming from God."[11] This description of God's ability to reign over creation while letting humans and angels and demons also have influence provides a general understanding of the Christian acceptance of God's sovereignty.

Some theologians will emphasise God at work in the lives of people more than others, but the broad recognition of God in charge above creation is consistent. This "aboveness" God has from creation is described by theologians as God's *transcendence;* God lives supreme above creation. Christians also affirm and emphasise that God is *holy*; God is separate and distinct from creation. Right alongside these two characteristics, Christians have the tension of affirming that God is *immanent*; God is near and present. This worldview of Christianity affirms that we have a relational God present among us, relating to us, while also existing above and separate from us. This personal God actively reveals descriptions and attributes to us, but it's important that we avoid adding our own ideas onto God that are not rooted in truth. Some sloppy theologians have ended up with descriptions that look more like Zeus or Shiva or perhaps themselves rather than the God of the Bible.

In God's Own Words

Fancy theological terms are helpful in knowing about the Christian God, but perhaps most helpful is the language God actually uses to describe who God is. Exodus 34:6-7 gives a clear description of the character of God: "And he passed in front of Moses, proclaiming, "The Lord, the Lord, the compassionate and gracious God, slow to anger, abounding in love and faithfulness, maintaining love to thousands, and forgiving wickedness, rebellion and sin. Yet he does not leave the guilty unpunished; he punishes the children and their children for the sin of the parents to the third and fourth generation." These features are worth giving attention to as this verse is one of the most quoted within the Bible itself by other biblical authors and provides the characteristics God chooses to help us understand the nature of God.

First listed is *compassionate*. This word Yahweh chooses as a self description speaks to the maternal care and powerful concern God has for humanity. In fact, The Bible Project theologians first bring up how the Hebrew word for compassion is connected to the word for "womb" in their language, linking the idea to a mother's care for her child. This deeply relational word ought to help us to connect God's character to our relationship with this personal, knowable, loving, trinitarian God. Compassion is meant to be experiential and interactive as God enters human lives with care and concern. We see this play out from the start of the covenantal relationship with Israel where God speaks to the people through the prophets and angelic messengers, listens to them through the priests and fervent prayers, and even fights off oppressive enemies or enacts restorative justice when the Israelites behave as oppressors. God's character is shown to be consistent in the revelation of Jesus who is moved to specific actions by feeling compassion - even describing it as the feelings of a mother hen longing to gather her chicks. Again, in the coming of the Holy Spirit described in Acts and through the epistles, we read that Christians are motivated to compassionate behaviors when filled and led by the Holy Spirit.

Grace is an often used and occasionally abused word in Christian circles. German theologian Dietrich Bonhoeffer is frequently referenced for his criticism of "cheap grace" in the church of his day that was quick to excuse bad behaviours in the name of grace. When God chooses the self description of *gracious*, this indulgent erasure of bad behaviour is not in mind. Rather, God shows favour with generosity to those who don't deserve it while acknowledging the seriousness or weightiness of the favour given. The New Testament explanations for grace are heavily linked with God's gift of salvation which shows how God is working to bring life from death to those who will receive it rather than to dismiss harm. Grace has more to do with receiving healing than license to harm.

Next, God claims to be *slow to anger* which comes from a Hebrew idiom related to a "long nose" which is opposite to the "hot nose" of people "burning with anger." We see this play out through the biblical narrative as God so values the free will instilled in people, that God waits a long time to intervene in the affairs of humans. Once God's patience is used up, the biblical writers describe how the humans are turned over to the consequences of their bad behaviours. This characteristic shows how God preserves humanity from the immediate negative consequences of our selfish or harmful choices and gives us time to repent and make things right on our own.

According to The Bible Project theologians, what we call *loyal love* is from a Hebrew word that combines the concepts of love, generosity, and enduring commitment together. There's not an exact English match to that all encompassing term, so when we talk about God's loyal love, we need to think bigger than what the word "love" on its own might bring up for English readers. Connecting to God's compassion, we see the characteristic of loyal love as a relational connection and ongoing commitment God has to all people. Often in the Bible we see examples of how God endures in showing loyal love when the people are undeserving — like when we receive God's grace despite our mistakes. Loyal love also relates to the previous characteristic of being slow to anger; we see God continue to extend loyal love to people who repeatedly fail and break their covenant promises.

This self description passage ends with *faithfulness* which similarly links with these ideas of God showing kindness and consistently offering good to humanity despite numerous failings. This word for faithfulness shows God's reliability in the face of an unstable world and fickle humans. Despite our lack of compassion, God will be faithful. Despite humanity's indulgence in selfish behaviours, God is faithful. Despite the oppression and injustice people enact, God is faithful. Despite our hate of others, God's faithful character is unwavering.

The last bit in the Exodus passage to be addressed here is the words God uses about punishment. Honestly, it would be easier to move on, but since the Bible never takes the easy way out, good theology shouldn't either. The idea of God as a punisher makes a lot of people uncomfortable, and unfortunately makes others a little too comfortable. Countless students of American literature have been subjected to the study of Jonathan Edwards' famous sermon titled "Sinners in the Hands of an Angry God." In recent years, theologian Brian Zahnd fought back against the imagery publishing a book titled *Sinners in the Hands of a Loving God*. This tension in theological debates can't be resolved in a paragraph. Instead, we can acknowledge that sin does matter to God; this verse indicates that punishment is a result of wrongdoing. We'll look at sin in chapter six, but knowing that God is not dismissive or forgetful of bad things matters in our worldview.

Conclusion

A significant feature not to be overlooked about the God of the Bible is that of creator. The opening chapters of Genesis prominently feature God as *creative*. While theologians differ on the authorship and dates even between the first two chapters as well as the methods by which God enacted the creation of the world, there is agreement that God is creative and involved in creation. Theologian Lisa Sharon Harper writes in her text *The Very Good Gospel*, "Genesis 2 offers an intimate narrative of creation. This is no sweeping epic poem. Instead, we see God get down into the muck... intimately involved in the creation of humanity."[12] This analysis emphasises how personal the creation of humanity is, but it also highlights the engagement God has in the creative process. From the first pages of the Bible, God is presented as creator and significantly creates humanity to participate in the ongoing creative work of stewarding the world. Reading the creation account at the start of the Bible lays out how God was thoughtful and purposeful in ordering creation which has loads of implications for how humanity has reason and purpose as well. God as Creator gives meaning to the world and our lives.

This leads to the last element covered in this brief chapter: God's *relational* nature. I end with this characteristic which I only mentioned above partially because it is the one that most clearly sets the God of the Bible apart from a deistic worldview that creates a higher power with great abilities. If you're going to distinguish the God of Christianity from other vague notions of a big "God" concept in secular culture that's powerful but uncaring, the relational element is most important. The other significant reason to conclude here is that if we skip over the fact that God deeply desires a personal relationship with us, it can lead people to recite facts about God without depending on God in any real way in their lives. Greg Boyd presents the danger in terms of a misguided theodicy when he writes,

"When asked what we think about God, we may recite all the orthodox attributes - love, omniscience, omnipotence - while entertaining a mental picture of God that is unloving and severely limited. Yet our actual picture of God, not our theoretical knowledge about God, most influences how we feel about him. It's impossible to enjoy a genuinely passionate and loving relationship with God when our mental picture of him doesn't inspire passionate love."[13]

You're reading a textbook right now that covers facts that Christians believe, but if you miss the part where facts influence lifestyle, worldview, and daily choices, it's not that great of a textbook. Pastors and Bible teachers are in danger of promoting deism or a misrepresentation of God if they fail to represent the God of the Bible as deeply relational while giving their lectures or sermons. As covered at the start of the chapter, God's trinitarian nature shows how God is relational with each person of the Trinity and invites humanity into that relationship as well. While in relationship with God, humans get to participate as stewards of creation while being co-creators in our lives as well. The following chapters on God the Son and God the Holy Spirit will show that very consistency of God's character that engages humanity relationally with all of these characteristics.

[1] This is one of the earliest statements of faith held by the Christian church which dates to somewhere in the fourth century.

[2] This is another largely ecumenical creed from 325 CE that is still affirmed by the overwhelming majority of Christian denominations.

[3] Mark 14:36, Luke 22:42

[4] John 14:16-17

[5] 1 Corinthians 14:33

[6] Matthew 28:19

[7] This Latin creed written and popularised in the sixth century deals primarily with doctrine surrounding the Trinity and the nature of Jesus in particular.

[8] Paul E. Little. *Know What You Believe* (Downers Grove: IVP Books, 2008), 44.

[9] 2 Kings 6:8-20

[10] Matthew 12:25, Luke 5:22

[11] Greg Boyd, *Is God to Blame?* (Downers Grove: IV Press, 2003), 90.

[12] Lisa Sharon Harper, *The Very Good Gospel* (Colorado Springs: Waterbrook, 2020), 40.

[13] Greg Boyd, *Is God to Blame?* (Downers Grove: IV Press, 2003), 21.

TWO

Jesus | Christology

and in Jesus Christ, His only Son Our Lord,
Who was conceived by the Holy Spirit, born of the
Virgin Mary, suffered under Pontius Pilate,
was crucified, died, and was buried.
He descended into Hell; the third day He rose
again from the dead;
He ascended into Heaven, and sits at the right
hand of God, the Father almighty; from thence
He shall come to judge the living and the dead.

This chapter centers on the doctrine of Christology - the person of Jesus Christ and his work in the universe. This topic has the most text dedicated specifically to it in the Apostle's Creed, and it stands as a central tenant of the Christian faith. All these words were put in for a reason, so we'll try to cover why each thing matters and how Christians think about Jesus. There is a lot of room for disagreement within Christianity, but the centre of the whole worldview is the person and work of Jesus Christ; he's kind of a big deal in Christianity. I use an analogy in my class shared by a friend: the Christian faith ought to be thought of as a target with Jesus Christ on the cross as the centre, and the further you move from that, the less important the issue is within Christianity. The concentric circles from the cross are the significant content agreed upon in the creeds, the major doctrines of the church, and finally opinions on liturgy, faith, and culture. The resurrection of Jesus is critical, but your understanding of women in church leadership is further from the cross and not a salvation issue; your preference of instruments in a church service are even less significant issues in your faith. The scope of this chapter is to cover the broad understanding of who Jesus is and how Christians relate to him as the second person of the Trinity. To keep centred on what theologians consider vital, we'll also look at a few well meaning scholars who veered a bit off course so that we don't follow them into heresy.

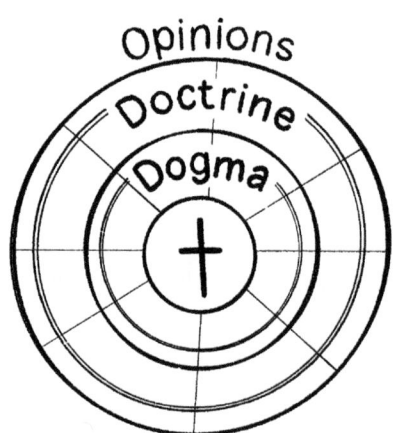

Jesus as God-Man

The first significant feature of Jesus is the paradox of him being fully God and fully man. Understanding Jesus clearly is key because Jesus is our closest picture of God as Jesus himself says he is God. Jesus brings light to our understanding of God's character as theologians reread the Old Testament seeing how he fulfilled prophecies and tangibly represented God's love, mercy, and forgiveness as spoken to the Israelites for centuries. Like the analogy from the previous chapter of the multidimensional God speaking through Scripture and historical connection with the Israelites, Jesus' incarnation was the most significant revelation of God's character; Jesus put on humanity while still remaining fully God so that we might know him better. Brad Jersak promotes the idea that Jesus is the clearest representation of God so we should read the whole Bible consistently, understanding the person and work of Jesus Christ as the best representation of God's character which reveals self sacrificing love and desire for relationship with humanity.

In the search for support of Jesus' eternal and divine nature, modern Aboriginal Anglican theologian Garry Deverell suggests, "Wisdom is both a witness and co-worker with God in the act of creating the universe, a master craftswoman at Yahweh's side. It is clear that many early Christian theologians understood this passage, and its sister passages in the apocryphal *Book of Wisdom*, as Jewish presentiments concerning Jesus Christ."[1] For two millennia, Christians have read through the Old and New Testament and seen a unified picture of Christ eternally existing but choosing to enter history as fully human.

Over the centuries of Christian history, theologians have argued over analogies emphasising one nature over the other, and church councils have subsequently condemned the heresies that diminish one of the natures at the expense of emphasising the other. It's worth running through the historical development of theology to see how carefully we've arrived at the orthodox defense of who Jesus has been eternally and continues to be. As we take a look through the thought process, remember these were not evil spies in the church planting corruption on purpose. Understanding the paradox of fully God and fully man is difficult to grasp but important enough to spend time thinking about carefully.

These debates about the dual nature of Jesus came early in the church and were centred in the Greek speaking world, so many of the terms theologians still use today are Greek words to indicate key features about Jesus. For example, the term "*homoousios*" is important in early documents to indicate that Jesus was of the same substance as God - fully divine. This was significant when Arius came around in the middle of the third century and claimed that Jesus' divine titles were just out of respect. Apollinaris was a contemporary of Arius who argued an opposite perspective, emphasising Jesus' divine nature at the expense of his humanity. Gregory of Nazianzus followed both of these controversial theologians a century later and wrote in support of the dual nature of Jesus that was affirmed again by church councils.

Arians today are considered outside of orthodoxy for their belief that Jesus was a created thing rather than fully equal to God the Father (and the Holy Spirit). *Ebonites* similarly emphasised Jesus' humanity at the expense of his divinity; this particular heresy claimed Jesus was an ordinary man who was just gifted by God. The *Apollinarian* view of Jesus concerned some as denying the full humanity in an overreaction to Arianism. This was not quite the same as Docetism which was an appealing view among Gnostics who thought the body and humanity was too tainted to be united with Jesus fully. *Docetism* was an early heresy that said Jesus was fully divine and came to live among humans while just appearing as human among us rather than having a full human nature. *Gnosticism* is an often occurring position that stems from a worldview that idolises Plato's view of the ideal; Gnostics generally think the body and material things are all bad, and that we should favour and pursue the more real "spiritual" elements of life that will last longer.

All these views were knocked down as failures to explain the *hypostatic union* - the fancy term theologians use to refer to the complicated way Jesus unites his human and divine natures. By and large, the early proponents of these ideas were not looking to corrupt the church; rather, these are examples of people who overreached in their explanations of this strange God-Man we call Jesus. Church history gives us healthy guardrails to keep us from losing sight of the element of paradox as we explain Jesus as fully God and fully man. Physicist and theologian John Polkinghorne compares the concept of the hypostatic union to the faith scientists have in quantum theory currently through his book *Quantum Physics and Theology*. His book compares how theologians search for answers knowing that Jesus is fully God and fully man though we cannot yet explain all the nuance of it just as physicists search for answers to explain quantum theory without full language for the nuance they know to be present. While keeping the names of these specific heresies locked in your brain is not vital, seeing the refinement of how Christians accept and reject explanations of the mystery of Christ matters for us today. If someone wants to faithfully hold a position within Christian orthodoxy and understand it fully, knowing the kinds of pitfalls that have tripped up thinkers in the past helps us have clear and cautious boundaries in what we do or don't say with regards to our beliefs.

When the early church members affirmed the phrases "conceived by the Holy Spirit" and "born of the Virgin Mary" they were affirming the full divinity and full humanity of this God-man who lived in history. The nod to Pilate anchors Jesus in the grand narrative of the Roman Empire as an actual person who interacted with real people rather than some mythological character. John Dominic Crossan is largely considered the academic expert on the historical Jesus; in his text on biblical literacy, he repeats the idea over and over that interpretation of the Bible ought to be anchored to the Christ of faith who is anchored to the Jesus of history. The biblical authors were explaining the theological reality of a historical figure. Church leaders carefully selecting the most important elements to include in the creeds also recognised this importance of worshipping Jesus Christ, the actual incarnation of God who entered into history as a full human.

Hypostatic Union	Jesus was both fully divine and fully human.
Heresy	Belief
Arian	Jesus was a created being, not equal to God
Ebonite	Jesus was an ordinary man, gifted by God.
Apollinarian	Jesus was more divine than he was human.
Docetist	Jesus was fully divine, only appearing human.

Jesus' Death and Resurrection

The creed also tells us that Jesus "was crucified, died, and was buried." There are theories to explain away the resurrection, and one of them relates to the suggestion Jesus wasn't dead when removed from the cross. Romans were the experts on death Count Rugen of *The Princess Bride* aspired to be; they would not have taken someone down from the cross who was even slightly alive. The biblical narrative tells of how the robbers crucified next to Jesus had their legs broken to ensure their death by crucifixion. Instead of having his legs broken, we read that Jesus had his heart stabbed. The description of a spear entering through the ribs and blood and water flowing separate is medically consistent with either a puncture of the heart and the clear protective fluid around the heart spilling separate from the blood or when the heart is punctured the blood platelets and plasma flowing separately. No one survives a spear popping their heart. This death is significant in Christian theology, and the resurrection matters because Jesus actually died.[2] Christians have various theories of atonement - what actually happened to make us right when Jesus died and rose again (which will be covered in chapter six). What Christians all agree on is that Jesus died and rose again, and that we all need Jesus in order to restore God's relationship with the broken people and creation.

Church history is decorated with extravagant paintings of what is called "the harrowing of hell" which is a theological description of Jesus descending into hell and setting free those who would have received his message of salvation but died before Jesus' own resurrection. Again, there is much dispute in the church on what happened during the days while Jesus was in the grave, but the emphasis the early church leaders put in the creeds is that Jesus descended to where the dead people go before rising back to life again. All Christians believe Jesus died; all Christians believe he rose again. Both beliefs are tied to other major doctrines in the church. Believing Jesus died matters in how Christians understand salvation being made available to humanity. Believing Jesus rose again is the lynchpin of the religion as Christians see it as not only validating what Jesus said in his life but also providing hope for the physical resurrection of Jesus followers in their final state.

The resurrection of Jesus changes people's lives. Starting with the first witnesses who went on to share this good news, live radically altered lives, and even often die for their beliefs, the New Testament stakes all of its weight on the resurrection. The apostle Paul even writes that Christians are most to be pitied in the world if the resurrection didn't happen.[3] This ongoing testimony of people changed by encounters with the resurrected Christ can be a valuable witness to the validity of belief in Christianity. What modern Jesus followers would describe as encounters with the risen Christ is in line with the creed's assertion that Jesus has now ascended into heaven according to the biblical narrative where he remains fully engaged in our physical world participating in a wider role through the spiritual reality. This active engagement is concurrent with the work of the Father and the Holy Spirit, affirmed as co-equal and co-eternal by the church.

Jesus' Return

The final major point this book covers is the belief that the church has in the return of Christ. This is a significant doctrinal point because it connects the Christian faith to the prophetic reality that the Old Testament describes the Messiah as both a suffering servant and a reigning king. This tension is balanced in the two arrivals of Jesus in Christian theology: first as the infant who grew up experiencing the fullness of humanity to die as the suffering servant and second as the reigning king in the fullness of his deity. Both messianic appearances involve the same Jesus as fully God and fully human, but his coming looks differently each time. We'll cover more about the second coming in chapter seven, but for now we need to emphasise the consensus among Christians that Jesus the Messiah is coming back.

This is a significant divergence in the messianic interpretations of the Old Testament from Jewish scholarship. In the Gospel narratives, many Jewish people reject Jesus as the Messiah because he did not come as the reigning king they expected, but there are also other long standing Jewish interpretations of the Lord sending a suffering messiah and a redeemer. Some of them include the belief that the nation of Israel collectively stands as the messiah for the world. Within that, some would say the Shoah (the Holocaust) of the 1940s was a corporate messianic endurance of evil endured by the people of Israel on behalf of the world. Other rabbis teach that a messiah comes once a century and there are micro cultural salvation experiences. While Christians have a wide range of interpretive expectations for Jesus' second coming (again, covered in chapter seven), there is general consensus that the Bible describes two messianic arrivals, both of which are Jesus, first as the first century humble arrival where he was crucified but conquered death followed by the anticipated final coming as righteous ruler.

[1] Garry Deverell, *Gondwana Theology* (Eugene: Wipf & Stock, 2019), 51.
[2] 1 Corinthians 15:3, 14
[3] 1 Cor 15:19

THREE

The Holy Spirit Pneumatology

I believe in the Holy Spirit

The Holy Spirit is one of the most polarising elements of Christian doctrine as some theologians overemphasise reliance on the ever present member of the Trinity and others deemphasise the ongoing role of the Holy Spirit to avoid reliance on misinterpreted emotions. In Kevin DeYoung's book on the Heidelberg Catechism, he opens his chapter on the Holy Spirit admitting, "Many Christians rarely think about the Holy Spirit."[1] His quick defence is there is more information in the New Testament about Jesus and God the Father than there is about the Holy Spirit. This is not, however, an excuse on his part for neglecting to learn about and relate to the Holy Spirit on the part of what he calls "traditional conservative Christians." Pentecostal denominations or charismatic theologians are often criticised on the other end of the spectrum as they speak of the Holy Spirit with little Scripture to back them up. As this text seeks to present what Christians agree on doctrinally, let's remember that there is universal consensus among Christians that the Holy Spirit is a full and equal member of the Trinity.

Because the Holy Spirit is so confusing, it's worth giving some broad strokes of agreement before diving into the myriad of nuances. Jesus refers to the Holy Spirit as a comforter and an advocate sent to teach us.[2] All Christians understand this significant role of the Holy Spirit, and they also look to Paul's lists of spiritual gifts and fruits of the spirit as special skills and character traits given and developed in all believers by the Holy Spirit.

Reference to the Holy Spirit is frequent in both the Old and New Testament. In the Hebrew text, the word *ruach* shows up on the first page as God creates. AJ Swoboda describes God stepping into the chaos to create beautifully in his book *Messy*:

Ruach is God's Spirit. In the story of Genesis, the Spirit, *Ruach*, hovers over this primordial chaos like a little girl ready to build and construct something majestic, helping to order it all to perfection. *Ruach* is all over the Bible. Throughout the rest of the Bible, there are many images of *Ruach*. A dove. Fire. Wind. Water. Cloud.[3]

Swoboda brings up later in his book how the Hebrew text uses a noun that has a feminine pronoun and the Greek word for spirit, *pneuma*, has a gender neutral pronoun. This trips up a lot of ordinary people and theologians alike engaging with the texts in English that assign masculine pronouns to the Holy Spirit. Some people absorb a masculine image of all three members of the Trinity through this translation which may or may not be harmful in their understanding of God. Others react to this information insisting upon feminine pronouns for the Holy Spirit celebrating it as a complement to the masculine pronouns for the Father and Son. To be clear, the Holy Spirit is not gendered in Scripture, but the personal pronouns are important rather than referring to the Holy Spirit as an impersonal "it" in English. Gendering the Holy Spirit through fights over pronouns often distracts from the work and relationship of the Holy Spirit to people today.

The Holy Spirit at Work

More significant and important is to identify the presence and work of the Holy Spirit in the Bible and through church history. As mentioned above, the Holy Spirit shows up on page one,[4] but we also see throughout the Old Testament vivid imagery to describe the Holy Spirit working among the people of Israel in particular. The highly symbolic language lends to various interpretations, but the consensus among Christian theologians is that the same Holy Spirit active in Genesis through Malachi came upon Mary to impregnate her and subsequently filled the first apostles and every subsequent believer in Jesus. This is a point where we can emphasise agreement among Christians that the Holy Spirit is not a new development as Christianity moved away from Judaism. Instead, all Christians affirm that eternal work and recognise the engagement humanity has had with the Holy Spirit both before and after Jesus enters history.

Theologians will most frequently cite the temporary nature of the visitation of the Holy Spirit in the Old Testament by quoting David praying that the Lord would not remove the Holy Spirit from him. There are certainly other examples of the temporary nature of the Holy Spirit coming upon people throughout the Old Testament. The interactions people have with the Holy Spirit are often unique and specific for a time or task. During the time of Moses there are stories of the Holy Spirit anointing people with leadership or prophetic ability to aid in governing this new nation wandering the desert; at the same time the Scripture describes how the Holy Spirit gave particular skill in embroidery to named individuals who were tasked with making the tabernacle tapestries.

The New Testament writers gave no indication that the interactions with the Holy Spirit that people had before would cease, but there were significant additions to the language and experience associated with the Holy Spirit post Pentecost. Pentecost is celebrated in church tradition fifty days after Easter and commemorates the event described early in Acts when the Holy Spirit arrived in tongues of fire on the heads of the gathered followers.[5] Concurrent to that physical description, the book of Acts says that they then spoke in other tongues.[6] This is another highly controversial and hotly debated doctrine within Christianity. Some believe that the metaphorical tongues of fire accompanied a one time miracle where the Holy Spirit gave the ability to speak in other languages or be understood by foreigners as a marker of the beginning of the church age. Others believe it is a record for the church of the first occurrence of the spiritual gift of tongues that still exists in various forms today. What Christians agree upon is that there is a distinct and real ongoing engagement with the Holy Spirit within the Christian church beginning at this moment in history.

All Christians still believe that the Holy Spirit seals[7] and indwells[8] those who profess belief in Jesus as Lord and wish to live following him. These special Christianese terms "seal" and "indwell" relate to the idea that Christians are marked, set apart, and made different by the presence of the Holy Spirit. Some believe this comes at the moment of recanting sin and asking for Jesus to forgive them while others believe the Holy Spirit waits to indwell people until the moment of a special baptism. This more charismatic leaning theological position sees a difference between water baptism as a profession of faith and spirit baptism as something often occurring with speaking in tongues. Speaking in tongues is not any kind of prerequisite to being a fully fledged Christian as a small number of denominations unfortunately promote. From the opposite end, it is also important to recognise that Scripture does affirm speaking in tongues as a gift of the Holy Spirit and should not be outright denied as an impossibility.

More charismatic denominations describe speaking in tongues as a prayer language, frequently using the term "glossolalia." More cautious denominations believe when Scripture describes the gift of tongues that it refers to the rare miracle of someone being able to speak to a person in another language they have never learned. Cessationist theologian R. A. Finlayson gives a clear definition of the two understandings of the gift of tongues though he strongly believed that was not a gift that continued in the modern church.

It is obvious that we must recognise two manifestations of the gift of tongues, the one conferring the ability to speak a recognisable language without having gone through the ordinary process of learning it, and the other leading certain disciples to speak in what was virtually a spiritual language that needed interpretation before its message could be conveyed to the hearers. This latter gift must be regarded as enabling the Spirit-filled disciples to dispense with ordinary language and to use the more direct medium of communication of the spiritual world.[9]

The unified affirmation of the church is that gifts of the Holy Spirit are real and intended for the edification of the church. The cessationist position affirms that the Holy Spirit miraculously gifted people with this ability to speak in tongues only in the past, and many more theologians fall in to the "open but cautious" camp with the understanding that while they have not seen genuine common manifestation of this gift, the Holy Spirit is indeed capable of granting it for the edification of the church in modern times. Charismatic denominations use the miraculous gifts of the Holy Spirit in a variety of ways in church services, discipleship, and personal prayer.

Kevin DeYoung brings up in his commentary on the Heidelberg Catechism, "Traditional conservative Christians know too little about, and cherish too lightly, the person and work of the Holy Spirit."[10] As a Christian within that category, he brings up that the caution comes from the fact that the Scriptures have much more to specifically say about God the Father and God the Son. While he falls quite comfortably in the conservative camp theologically, DeYoung does highlight key features of the Holy Spirit affirmed by all Christians as he describes the full divinity and present work of the Holy Spirit. Furthermore, DeYoung gives three benefits of the Holy Spirit found in Scripture that all Christians recognise: our share in Christ and his blessings as followers of Jesus, the comfort of the Holy Spirit, and the ongoing presence of the Holy Spirit. Christians of various denominational backgrounds will have more comfort describing the blessings of the Holy Spirit as "fruit" or "gifts" based on lists in Scripture or perhaps naming them as specific life experiences. Similarly, the diversity of language comes as Christians describe the comfort or presence of the Holy Spirit in personal experiences. Many are cautious in attributing peaceful feelings as the presence of the Holy Spirit while others are taught to name that frequently as the Holy Spirit at work in a personal way.

Other Spiritual Beings

While Christians talk about God as spirit, there are also other spiritual beings within the Christian worldview that are distinct and separate categories. The Old Testament in particular references many kinds of spiritual beings both good and evil. In the range of good or on the side of God, we read about the Divine Council as well as specific kinds of angels with various roles like messengers or warriors or those assigned to worship God on his throne. In Greg Boyd's careful theodicy *Is God to Blame?*, he asserts that angels also must have some measure of free will in their obedience to God's commands or in how they fulfil their duties. This proposes many questions which Christians must be cautious in providing speculation or answers. While many verses in the Bible do reference angels and even describe them in various ways - covered in eyes or covered in wings or as terrifying warriors - there are many details omitted by the biblical authors. We have reference to a couple specifically named angels who spoke with humans while other places just refer to the angelic messenger without a name. Some descriptions in the Bible reference angelic armies or large choirs singing God's praise when other stories include just a single spiritual being at work. Prophets like Ezekiel and John (who wrote Revelation) gave more physical descriptions while different biblical authors left out any characteristics for us to have a clear picture of the spiritual being with whom another biblical character interacts.

While curiosity may lead to creative depictions, there are a handful of clear, consistent facts about angels that Christians find in the Bible. First, they are on God's side. Significantly, they are not divine despite having more strength or abilities than humans do. Additionally, while angels are spiritual beings, they can at some times and places be made visible to humans. Perhaps our most important feature in the Christian worldview, Christians believe angels are *not* mediators between God and humans; humans have direct connection to God.

Demons, or evil spiritual beings, are equally intriguing to many people, and there ought to be great caution when engaging with demonic activity. All Christians affirm the existence of demonic forces though the frequency and experience varies widely. Most notably, in modern Western theology, "Satan" is frequently described as the fallen archangel Lucifer who led a revolt in heaven and now is the leader of all evil spiritual beings. Hebrew scholars are quick to point out that "satan" is just a word meaning "accuser" and perhaps the Satan in Scripture refers to a class of spiritual beings who stand as the accusers of humanity before God.

The Bible Project creators provide even more details about the spiritual beings described in the Bible in their seven video series on YouTube. They include details of how the biblical authors thought of the spiritual beings based on their cultural perspective. The overview, however, consistently fits the modern Christian affirmations of the existence and position of angels and demons.

[1] Kevin DeYoung, *The Good News We Almost Forgot* (Chicago: Moody Publishers, 2010), 103.
[2] John 14:26
[3] AJ Swoboda, *Messy* (Grand Rapids: Kregel Publications, 2012), 25.
[4] Genesis 1:2
[5] Acts 2:1-3
[6] Acts 2:4
[7] Ephesians 1:13
[8] 1 Corinthians 3:16, Romans 8:9
[9] R. A. Finlayson, *Reformed Theological Writings* (Ross-shire: Mentor, 1996), 121.
[10] Kevin DeYoung, *The Good News We Almost Forgot* (Chicago: Moody Publishers, 2010), 103.

FOUR

The Church
Ecclesiology

---

the holy catholic Church

Before any protestant readers panic, the word "catholic" in this creed is not capitalised because it is referring to the general church, not to the specific denomination. Before any Catholic readers panic, since Vatican II, Catholics have accepted those in other Christian denominations as what they call "separated brethren." It's not a perfect unity experienced in reality, but this textbook serves as an ecumenical look at Christian theology which means it covers perspectives across a wide range of denominations. This chapter will inevitably highlight several differences in both belief and practice, but the greater emphasis is on what brings the church together in affirmation and purpose. It's hard not to see what separates denominations before what unites all Christians, but keep in mind this book covers the range of things all Christians affirm while looking at the diversity among different branches of the faith.

When the early church began gathering after Jesus' ascension, it was a fast growing sect of Judaism. This is why the holy book of Christianity, the Bible, includes both the Scriptures of Judaism (which Christians call the Old Testament) in addition to writings of the first century Jesus followers that lean heavily on the Jewish tradition (which Christians call the New Testament). In fact, all but one of the attributed New Testament authors is Jewish.[1] As Scottish theologian R. A. Finlayson notes in his *Reformed Theological Writings*, "Though the New Testament is normative, it is not to be studied in isolation"[2] which is an encouragement to look at the New Testament in light of the culture and context of the Old Testament - Judaism. A basic familiarity with Jewish tradition, particularly as it was practiced by Jesus and his first followers, is critical to understanding the practices of the modern church. Another vital element of understanding the wide diversity of the Christian church today is by having an overview of the now two thousand year history that has seen the development and destruction of certain rites and rituals in addition to how the church has held fast to the most central beliefs and behaviours. Without getting too caught up in the disagreements, this chapter will try to cover how Christians prioritised certain beliefs and behaviours from the start and developed unique different expressions along the way.

The Earlier Church

The book of Acts provides the initial history of how this rapidly expanding group quickly began leaving Jewish religious communities, integrating foreigners, and setting up gatherings in large homes. For the first few hundred years, Christianity rapidly expanded across the Roman Empire, and in the early centuries, leaders from various countries and cultures gathered to affirm key beliefs and discuss growing problems. While the Apostle's Creed (which this textbook takes its outline from) was one of the most widely agreed upon statements of faith, the first major church split happened in the fifth century when Christians who affirmed the singular nature of Jesus felt the decisions made at Chalcedon in 451 CE moved away from the rejection of Nestorianism.[3] The Chalcedon Christology was trying to emphasise the dual nature of Jesus, but the break away adherents are who we recognise as the Oriental Orthodox Churches today. Among them, the Coptic Christians most prevalent in Africa are now thought of as a Christian denomination rather than an entirely different religion. The complicated story of political power and plagues tied up in this first split of the church go beyond the scope of this textbook, but don't lose sight of the unity that all Christians - even after this major disagreement - were affirming the basic doctrines covered here.

Six hundred years passed before the next major break in the church which had the mutual excommunication of the eastern and western churches from each other in 1054 CE. While several theological differences strengthened the split, the primary issue was the Latin branch adding a single word to their creeds explaining their understanding that the Holy Spirit proceeds from the Father *and from the Son*. The Eastern church was scandalised at the implication of a lower ranking of the Holy Spirit through some hierarchy or succession in this wording. This split became what we now recognise as the Roman Catholic Church and the Eastern Orthodox Church. There are smaller distinctions within the Eastern Orthodox tradition, but it was another half a millennium before the Roman Catholic Church was the focus of the next major splintering of the church. Once more, let's not forget despite these differences, all churches were doing their best to honestly follow Jesus in their local gatherings. Historians examining the eastern and western branches will both quickly find political agents working to use religion as a weapon of power. Constantine is perhaps the most notable name among those who converted to Christianity and used it for political gain. His adoption of Christianity as the religion of the Roman Empire simultaneously shared the Good News of Jesus with countless people and opened the floodgates for political corruption into the church hierarchy.

By the 1500s, many faithful leaders within the Catholic Church were frustrated and disturbed by the corruption that had gained a strong foothold and wanted to restore the Bride of Christ to a more faithful representation on earth. Among the more famous are reformers like Martin Luther, Ulrich Zwingli, John Calvin, John Wycliffe, and William Tyndale. Scores of others in the centuries both before and after them laboured to work reforms from within the Catholic church and either found such resistance they left voluntarily or they were excommunicated. Hundreds of denominations cropped up in the centuries after these bright stars in history, but there were also many reformers who remained within the Roman Catholic tradition attempting to make positive changes from the inside. Most notably, Martin Luther considered Erasmus of Rotterdam a partner in reform until Luther was excommunicated and Erasmus chose to remain faithful to the Roman Catholic Church and use his influence from within to point people to Jesus.

If you check the publication date of this book, the church is due for another upheaval. Theologians with their eyes open may already see it, but it's far beyond the scope of this text. While there is a lot that divides and distinguishes denominations, there are more important issues that unite the Christian church across denominations. The starting point in looking at the church should always be the things that unite different gatherings. The unity is around the profession of faith in the person and work of Jesus Christ of Nazareth. To be sure, the details of how some churches describe Jesus may differ, but all of them unite around this central figure as fully God and fully man, eternal in the Godhead who came to earth in the incarnation taking on full humanity to live, die, and rise again to restore relationship between humanity and God.

Sacraments

From the earliest gatherings of the church, this profession of faith in Jesus and receiving of salvation through him was the central feature of becoming a Christian. It would always, however, accompany some kind of life transformation. The book of Acts narrates how people lived differently based on this profession of faith. The biblical account tells numerous stories of people receiving the Holy Spirit and living more generous lives marked by the love, joy, peace, and other fruits of the Holy Spirit. These features remain valid indicators of active participation in the Christian church though some other gatherings have formalised professions of faith and participation in the special rites called sacraments of the church. Many protestant denominations avoid the term "sacrament" in preference for less confusing language. The official term holds a connotation of a holy or sacred thing, but many Christians would just say it's a special action that indicates some level of participation or membership in the church.

While the Roman Catholic denomination defines seven separate sacraments, there are just two that are more widely recognised as distinct sacraments among most Christian denominations.[4] The first sacrament practised among all denominations in some form is baptism which is often considered a mark of entry into the church. All churches use this as a symbolic washing of the participant in water to enact the cleansing from sin that happens when we receive salvation from Jesus. The practice of baptism itself did not begin with the Christian church. The Bible talks about John the Baptist who encouraged his Jewish followers to symbolically wash themselves clean of their old habits and live in a renewed commitment to honour God with their lives. Jesus himself was baptised by John and subsequently encouraged his disciples to baptise those who commit to following him. Over the centuries, the church has developed how this practice happens. For example, when the church was still very young, new converts were generally adults who, in their decision to be washed clean of their sinful lives, would separate by gender and be baptised naked. This gave way to more public baptisms where participants wore white robes to symbolise how they were now clothed in righteousness unstained by their sin.

Some denominations practice infant baptism (sometimes called paedobaptism) which is done as an act of faith that the child will be raised in a Christian home and come to accept salvation on their own later in life, usually followed by a confirmation service when the young person chooses to be a part of the church. Eastern Orthodox churches do their infant baptisms as three quick immersions while Roman Catholic, Anglican, Lutheran, and others more commonly do infant baptisms with a sprinkling of water on the infant's head. Within each of these denominations, there is a lot more nuance to the implications of what happens through the sacrament. Focusing here on the similarities, we see that these churches value the practice as an important part of inclusion in the church.

Widely practised full immersion baptisms through other protestant denominations may sometimes involve a brief course covering the beliefs of the Christian faith or simply a profession of faith on the part of the believer. Some churches will have a pastor involved in dipping the person into the water with words recognising their profession of faith in addition to something regarding the symbolic death to their old self and resurrection into new life in faith. An even larger number of Christians choose to have a significant member of their faith journey as the person who baptises them. While there is an extreme diversity of presentations, the commonality among Christian churches is to have an intentional, public declaration of faith that symbolically shows the death to or washing of sin in the person followed by the resurrection or cleansed life that follows as a member of the church.

The second sacrament that is present in some form in every Christian church is that of communion. Sometimes called "Eucharist" or "The Lord's Supper," this sacrament involves the recognition of Jesus' command that we remember his sacrifice until he returns. This was first enacted with Jesus among his disciples just before his crucifixion. Jesus first gives them bread and tells them it represents his body broken for them; next he shares wine and says it symbolises his blood shed for them. He tells his closest followers to do this repeatedly in remembrance of him until his return. The symbolic sharing of bread and wine deliberately echoes the Jewish betrothal covenant practice contemporary to Jesus. Faithful Jewish couples would agree to a marriage contract during a meal that included the sharing of bread and wine. The groom would then go prepare a home for his bride while she remained in the house of her father learning and preparing to be a good wife. When Jesus shared this last meal with his followers,[5] he drew strong connections between this betrothal ceremony as he told them to eat and drink these things as an ongoing reminder that he would return for them. The New Testament writers and Christian theologians frequently capitalise on this metaphor of the church as the bride of Christ. Christians continue to take communion as this remembrance of betrothal and commitment to Christ in addition to anticipation of Jesus' return.

Theologians depart in the nuanced understanding of what happens the moment believers gather to take communion in addition to the means and methods in which it ought to be taken. The first distinction is "open table" versus "closed table" communion. Most theologians hold that communion is a special thing that only Jesus followers ought to participate in. Because of this, some churches have requirements to demonstrate that you are in good standing with the church denomination before participating in their communion portion of the service which would be considered a "closed table" understanding of communion. Some churches may only allow people to participate in communion after their baptism or confirmation. Orthodox and Catholic churches specifically reserve communion for those who are members of their specific denomination in addition to having confessed and repented of sins before taking communion.

A couple of notable moments of this throughout history were during the reformation of the 1500s when some priests refused to offer communion to those who they believed were publicly living in sin or believing heresy - therefore not in good standing with the church. Within the last century, several Catholic priests made headlines for key refusals to politicians who publicly go against certain church beliefs. At the time of this writing, discussions are happening amongst theologians about how this sacrament is at risk of becoming a political weapon. The official position of the church is about Jesus rather than political policies, though Christians have often considered seriously how their religious beliefs affect their concern and engagement in their government or politics in various ways.

The weightiness of receiving communion within the Catholic church relates to more than just the belief it is a holy sacrament. Catholic doctrine affirms that the wafer and wine transform into the body and blood of Jesus Christ which is significant in salvation and ought not to be wasted on those actively living against how the church believes Jesus tells us to. This belief in the transformation of the elements used in the Eucharist is called "transubstantiation" because they believe the actual substance has been transformed. This was reaffirmed by the Roman Catholic church during the thirteenth session of the famous Council of Trent which ended in October 1551.[6]

The reformers of the sixteenth century spent a lot of time rethinking this understanding of what happened during the Lord's Supper. Some of them, notably Martin Luther, thought that transubstantiation was an unnecessary and unbelievable attempt to explain the mystery of the Eucharist. His explanations instead chose to explain that while the substance of the elements themselves were unchanged, there was a very real presence of Jesus invited by the celebrant during the Lord's Supper. This position is referred to as "consubstantiation" and places the emphasis on the *real presence* of Christ when taking communion though the elements remain unchanged. Luther's contemporary Ulrich Zwingli is perhaps the best known reformer who held the memorial position arguing that Jesus' words about his body and blood were metaphorical and the emphasis was on the remembrance of Jesus' actions. To Zwingli, the "real presence" was an unnecessary theological point; communion was important because Jesus told us to do it, but it was only a reminder rather than a mystical event.

Due to these varying approaches to communion, churches differ on who is allowed to give the elements of communion, what they are, and how they ought to be distributed. Those that practice what is called a "high church" liturgy will have a more specific structure of a pastor or trained leader of the church bless the elements - most frequently specially made wafers and wine - before participants come individually to receive the elements. The blessing is usually through a written prayer that acknowledges each element following an order that is intentional and symbolic. The container and chalice holding the bread and wine are both placed on a white cloth to bless them; water is added to the wine as an intentional theological reference to the water that flows separate from Jesus' body on the cross after his death. As each participant receives the elements, they are told, "This is Christ's body broken for you; this is Christ's blood shed for you." The details of the service are meant to be specific reminders of theological truths rather than blind ritual.

There is much more diversity in practice among what are considered "low church" liturgical services. Communion is no less important to these Christians, but it looks significantly less formal in the presentation. Many of these churches have any member of the church pass out plates with bread or crackers and individual tiny cups of wine or grape juice and a church member or pastor may lead the congregation in a prayer or words of reflection before everyone either takes the elements together or after a brief personal prayer. Some of these denominations even encourage smaller gatherings of members to take communion more frequently together; Christians on the farther end of memorialism may choose to use any food and drink as substitutes for bread and wine to intentionally remember the sacrifice of Jesus' body and blood. The unity across denominations is the centrality of remembering Jesus' death and sacrifice as he asked his followers to do. This critical practice of the church has looked different through the centuries but remained a vital sign of a Christian gathering.

What the Church Does

Other practices central to the early church were fellowship, prayer, acts of service, and sharing their faith. The implementation of these key elements quickly adapted as the church spread through different cultures and became established institutionally over time. There are a whole lot of things that mark Jesus' followers through history. Most significant however, as defined by Scripture, is that Jesus followers are recognised by their love. It is an act of love for Christians to pray - both sharing their honest emotions, concerns, and thanksgiving with God while also listening and responding to promptings from the Lord. It is an act of love to God and others to provide needed services to the marginalised or the neighbour. It is an act of love also within the Christian worldview to invite others into the community of faith.

The fellowship feature may be the most critical to the function and purpose of the church, however. Christians believe that the church is meant to represent and do the work of Jesus in the world. This sharing of one another's burdens is seen through history as Jesus followers provide tangible help to the poor in addition to emotional support to the struggling. Scripture is positively littered with commands to care for others as an act of worship to God.[7] There are also strong commands for Christians to care for creation,[8] and the global church follows that command in diverse ways across local gatherings. Any Christian church would quickly grant that the building or weekly meeting is not the church itself but rather a stopping point or a momentary collection of the living and breathing body of Christ spread out across the world and through history. What unifies the church, then, is the belief in the same God who came in the form of Jesus to reconcile and restore relationship with humanity as revealed through the Bible. Disputes over the order of the service or time of the gatherings may arise, but emphasis remains on the enactment of loving God and loving others.

[1] Luke, the named author of the Gospel of Luke and the book of Acts, was a Gentile convert to Christianity. A doctor and historian, he travelled with the apostle Paul on part of his missionary journeys and wrote an extended record of the life of Jesus and the history of the early church.

[2] R. A. Finlayson, *Reformed Theological Writings* (Ross-shire: Mentor, 1996), 153.

[3] This term generally refers to a belief that separated the divine and human natures of Jesus which was first associated with fifth century theologian Nestorius.

[4] The five additional sacraments of the Catholic church are confirmation, reconciliation, anointing of the sick, marriage, and holy orders.

[5] Jesus initiated this practice during the Passover meal, and the connection between Passover in the Jewish tradition and communion in the Christian tradition is also significant.

[6] Alistair McGrath, *Historical Theology* (Blackwell: Oxford, 1998), 196.

[7] Ecclesiastes 4:9-12, Acts 20:35, Galatians 6:2

[8] Genesis 2:15

FIVE

People Anthropology

---
the communion of saints

The Apostle's Creed uses this phrase "communion of saints" to refer to those who are in an active relationship with the church,[1] but the general doctrine of humanity covers those people who are also outside the faith. All Christians affirm that people are made in the image of God and that we are part of the community of believers based on our acceptance of relationship with God. Christians do distinguish those who choose to follow Jesus and those who do not, but historically, Christians show love and care to people of all faith backgrounds; that is one of the most effective evangelistic tools - to the annoyance of many religious and political leaders throughout history. Before the Roman Empire became overtly favourable to Christians post-Constantine, many leaders noted with some annoyance how the subversive Christians cared for the poor and marginalised of all faith backgrounds. The Jesus followers were disruptive enough to be noticed for their worship of Jesus over Caesar, but they were annoyingly good citizens in many other respects going out of their way to care for others.

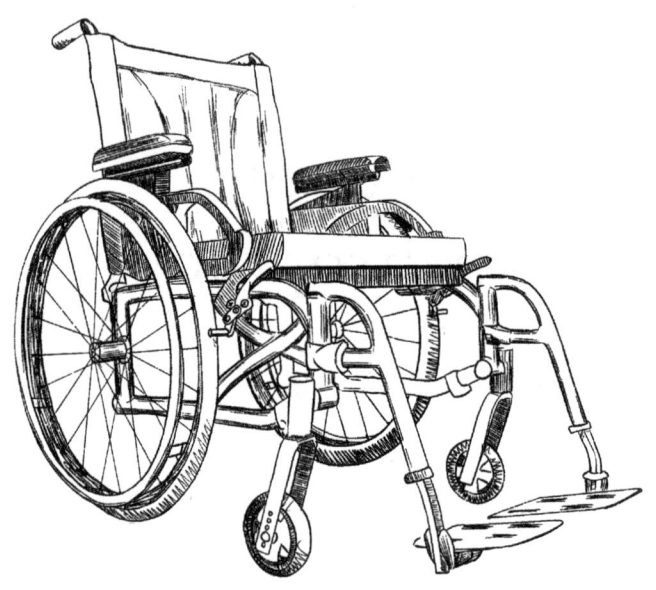

Imago Dei

Additional nuance in the doctrine of humanity comes in the definitions of "image of God" and what a right relationship with God looks like. This matters so that the actual inclusion of all diverse people as God intends is not twisted into erasing differences. The global church is a beautiful mosaic, and we need to look at all the different cultures and celebrate their differences while identifying the features that unite us as the human race. While on the surface Christians are quick to say all people are people, there have been notable failures to treat all people equally even within the church. We're focusing in this book on the inclusion of all people as made in the image of God by looking at some minority theologians who eloquently express their full humanity.

Within the study of humanity in Christian theology, the Latin phrase "imago dei" is dominant; this term meaning "image of God" comes from Genesis 3, and several different definitions crop up in Christian writings. Theologians are quick to emphasise that the phrase "image of God" ought never be confused with humans made to look like God. This is important in our concept of God as spirit, but it also carries implications even beyond thinking of God according to one race but in how we still view the disabled community as made in the image of God. In Stephanie Tait's "A Liturgy for Disability" included in a collection of thoughts on prayer, she writes,

Convict us, Lord, of the ways we have harmed those who are disabled with our belief, whether spoken or unspoken, that they may be experiencing punishment for sin. Teach us like you did your disciples, saying, 'Neither they nor their parents have sinned. This happened so that God's mighty works might be displayed in them.'[2]

This passage illuminates how the church has often looked over the full humanity of those who have limited ability. The exclusion of those with physical or mental disability from full participation in the church is a disturbing shortcoming. Theologians at their best, however, look to definitions of the image of God that will be inclusive of all people. Whatever it means to be in God's image, it cannot be limited to intelligence at the exclusion of the mentally impaired, and it cannot be limited to ability or function at the exclusion of the physically impaired.

Clearly the image of God cannot be defined by our appearance, ability, or intelligence. Rather than a series of definitions of what it is not, however, there is one helpful feature Christian theologians widely acknowledge: whatever it means to be made in the image of God, it has to do with relationship. In the Genesis narrative, God speaks in what many theologians refer to as Trinitarian language by using "us" and "our" in the wording about creating humanity and wanting a relationship with this particular created thing.[3] Some theologians like Richard Rohr interpret Russian painter Andrei Rublev's famous icon of the Trinity as specifically indicating the mutual relationship between the members of the Trinity while also intentionally creating space and invitation to the viewer into relationship with the Trinity. Reformed Scottish R. A. Finlayson (from a far different interpretive perspective than Catholic Rohr) says, "Since God is within Himself a fellowship, then His moral creatures are built on the same fellowship pattern, and they find fullness of life only within fellowship... Christian fellowship is therefore the divinest thing on earth, the most like the life of God."[4] This broad recognition of relationship as central to the human experience crosses boundaries of ethnicity, gender, and class.

All Nations and Races

The message Paul delivers in the epistles[5] describing how all are equal in Christ is often used to erase differences in ethnic identity or even gender and class. When Eric Mason responds to this particular misuse of Galatians 3:28[6] in his critique of an identity cult who call themselves "Hebrew Israelites," he deftly asserts, "What this verse is really saying is that ethnicity, social status, and gender don't give any of us a leg up in our relationship with God. We are all fallen and need to place our trust in Jesus for salvation."[7] This quote comes from Mason's essay included in his edited collection of apologetic works particularly aiming to restore Black dignity with the Gospel. His introduction and early chapters assert this is only necessary because of a history of demeaning or belittling Black people. Unfortunate backlash to these kinds of texts comes from the similar misuse of the Galatians passage. Theologian Jerome Gay's chapter in Mason's edited work combats this criticism:

They argue that race doesn't matter. This argument not only reveals their assumption that their version of history and their anthropological experience is universal and therefore applies to everyone, but it also fails to acknowledge that they've used race in their favour to paint the Bible and Christian history largely white.[8]

As this current textbook chapter looks at the Christian doctrine of people across all cultures and time, it's important to note the tensions that have developed in giving full dignity to all people that run through major denominations. Anglican Aboriginal theologian Garry Deverell addresses that tension in his slim volume *Gondwana Theology* which includes reflections on the racism he's endured as someone of Trawloolway descent.[9] He first lays out that racism is evil because God wants community with all people and uses Jesus to enter the human story and rebuke our inhumanity towards each other. He continues,

Racism is evil, finally, because it will not have the last word. The last word is love, the love shared between the Father and the Son in the power of the Holy Spirit, a love that is always going out of itself in creative and hospitable action ... In the work of Christ and the giving of his Spirit, every sin is both forgiven and forgotten and the idea that someone might be used and abused because of their ethnicity has become absolutely laughable. Racism is evil, in summary, because God is a trinity, a threefold relation of divine equals who go out towards one another and toward the cosmos in love and mercy. In this story and this grammar is the indispensable plumbline of care and regard and justice ... for the church, for human society, and for the whole of creation.[10]

Deverell's criticism of racism comes from several theological points, and it beautifully shows how Christian theology is upholding the dignity of all people. He writes from the experience of mixed ancestry of native people who were abused and oppressed and colonisers who invaded and inflicted harm on other image bearers. His perspective is valuable as he writes theology within the Anglican tradition that is distinctly for Australian Jesus followers. Borrowing names of native species and landmarks in his liturgical prayers, Deverell compares his practice to the way psalmists and other biblical writers used metaphors immediately recognisable to their initial audience. While Hebrew poets wrote to an audience familiar with habits of sheep and mountain lions, Deverell can reference the patterns of quokka and kangaroos that his congregation recognise locally. This particular theological method deftly partners the universality of Christian truths with the cultural uniqueness of a specific people group. *Ecumenical* theology, theology across denominations, at its best will do this as it seeks to hold fast to key truths and celebrate the diversity of expressions in different places. Eric Mason and Garry Deverell are modern Jesus followers actively looking to honour their uniqueness as members of humanity while thinking and communicating well about the important doctrines of the Christian faith.

All Men and Women

A great deal of damage can come from limiting the humanity of another by ethnicity. Similar damage has been done in how Christians understand and express the fullness of humanity between male and female. Many modern female theologians are rejected from wider Christian circles because of the interpretations of a few key texts in the Bible that lead them to believe women ought not to instruct men in theology or anything else.[11] There is legitimate tension in the interpretation of the texts, but theologians of all positions ought to be cautious to ground their positions and explanations in language that affirms the full humanity of both men and women. Sadly, a number of church fathers and modern theologians carried misogynistic language into their interpretations of texts like Genesis 3 condemning Eve as the root of evil. In her book chronicling a journey to live according to literal interpretations of gender norms and expectations for wives and women described in the Bible, Rachel Held Evans concludes,

I've watched congregations devote years and years to heated arguments about whether a female missionary should be allowed to share about her ministry on a Sunday morning, whether students older than ten should have female Sunday school teachers, whether girls should be encouraged to attend seminary, whether women should be permitted to collect the offering or write the church newsletter or make an announcement... all while thirty thousand children die every day from preventable disease. If that's not an adventure in missing the point, I don't know what is."[12]

Ultimately, the Christian worldview affirms the dignity and humanity of men and women, charging all people equally to advocate for the widows and the orphans, the oppressed and the marginalised.

As humans, we inherently know we are set apart from creation, but we sometimes struggle to engage with both creation and others well. Theologian Lisa Sharon Harper affirms this in her book *The Very Good Gospel* when she writes,

We are made in God's likeness, but we are not God. We are well aware that there are only two kinds of beings, creature and Creator. We are creature. God is God; we are not. Therefore, we are not free to do as we please with creation. Our dominion must bow to the will of God. And if it is to be in the image of God's dominion, then it must be grounded in love. Love binds all creation together."[13]

This struggle to steward creation is aided by a focus on love. Christians have made better progress with this at various points in history. Some denominational movements have even been primarily identified by their social justice engagement as Christians seek to recognise the full humanity of those on the margins of society. Charitable works, however, are not a requirement to be a Christian. Instead, church history shows they are a frequent and common outpouring of those whose lives are transformed by Jesus. The affirmation of the humanity of those who look differently, live differently, or spend their money differently is what is central to the Christian faith, and the church is historically most effective in its mission when it loves people across these various borders.

[1] In this context, "communion" doesn't have any connection to the sacrament; this is just a reference to membership in the global church.

[2] Stephanie Tait, "A Liturgy for Disability," *A Rhythm of Prayer* (Convergent Books: Colorado Springs, 2021), 79.

[3] Genesis 1:26

[4] R. A. Finlayson, *Reformed Theological Writings* (Mentor: Ross-shire, UK, 1996), 32.

[5] Letters written to churches included in the New Testament.

[6] "There is neither Jew nor Greek, there is neither slave nor free, there is no male and female, for you are all one in Christ Jesus." (Galatians 3:28 ESV)

[7] Eric Mason, "Engaging Hebrew Israelites," *Urban Apologetics: Restoring Black Dignity with the Gospel* (Zondervan Reflective, 2021), 92.

[8] Jerome Gay, Jr., "All White Everything," *Urban Apologetics: Restoring Black Dignity with the Gospel* (Zondervan Reflective, 2021), 18.

[9] Deverell traces his ancestry from both colonizers of Australia as well as indigenous Aboriginal people from the Traloolway tribe that inhabited the island of Tasmania.

[10] Garry Deverell, *Gondwana Theology* (Eugene: Wipf & Stock, 2019), 55.

[11] This is most clearly in 1 Timothy 2:11-12 though Ephesians 5:23-35, Titus 2:3-5, and 1 Peter 3:7 are frequently used in theological debate surrounding this topic.

[12] Rachel Held Evans, *A Year of Biblical Womanhood* (Thomas Nelson: Nashville, TN, 2012), 255.

[13] Lisa Sharon Harper. *The Very Good Gospel* (WaterBrook: Colorado Springs, CO, 2020) 105.

SIX

Sin & Salvation Hamartiology & Soteriology

---
the forgiveness of sins

Sin is an ugly and overused word. It has a long history, and the word we translate from the Hebrew originally was related to archery and missing the target. By the time Jesus was walking around speaking Aramaic, the concept of sin was connected not only to owing a debt but to broken relationships with others. When Lisa Sharon Harper explains how the author of Hebrews likely uses the term we translate as sin, she writes,

In Hebrew culture, sin has more to do with the break between relationships than with individual imperfection. It was about love and the lack of it. Original hearers likely understood the text as 'Let us also lay aside every weight and the separation that clings so closely.'[1]

Christian theologians will all agree the relationship element of sin is significant though the descriptions and definitions still widely vary. Students have come through my classes having heard over and over the simplistic and somewhat misleading definition of sin as "anything that makes God sad." This does a discredit to the other relational damage that comes with most things defined as sin.

The Jewish concept of sin that connected the idea to missing the mark implied there was a mark to hit - a target of right living. Now the concept of sin still includes the idea there is a right way to live, but it expands to also recognise that failing to live rightly causes harm to others - God, people, even the land around us. Christians agree on this, and they agree that all people sin. The divergence begins right after that - some theologians say we are born in sin we inherited all the way back from the moment Adam and Eve chose to sin while others say we *inevitably* choose sin at some point just like all people since the start of the human race. Kevin DeYoung explains the former position in line with the Heidelberg Catechism saying, "We are born with a warped nature, tainted with an inherent and inherited corruption from conception on."[2] His theological position is close to Augustine telling the church that babies are born in sin.[3] Those theologians describe that we literally inherit sin as part of our conception saying, "Adam transmitted to his posterity... because of the unity of the human race."[4] Some theologians carried that interpretation to the extreme that babies go to hell when they die if they aren't yet baptised. This position has caused a lot of tension through church history and led to the development of the "age of accountability" theory that we are not held accountable for sins until we are old enough to know the weight of our decisions. DeYoung and many other theologians in his camp do not get hung up on this, however. Their focus is on the hope we have in Jesus who saves us from this sin we are born into. The inherited initial state of being marred by sin is not the end of the story. Interestingly, it is the staunchly reformed theologian R. A. Finalyson who gives a very firm rebuttal to the idea of inherited sin. When describing how Jesus being initially sinless is imperative to his full humanity, Finlayson includes this defence: "Sin was an intrusion from without that made man less than man, with a heart of stone rather than a heart of flesh."[5] From this quote, clearly, the idea of inherited sin or belief that sin is inevitable does not fall neatly into reformed or progressive theological camps.

Theory	Beliefs about Atonement
Christus Victor	Jesus won a battle against Satan.
Satisfaction Theory	Jesus satisfied our debt to God.
Moral Influence	Jesus restored our relationship with God.
Socinian Theory	Jesus was provided by God as a perfect example for humanity.
Mystical	We cannot fully understand atonement.
Governmental	God is a righteous judge and needed payment for the sin of humanity. Jesus makes things right with his death.
Penal Substitutionary Atonement	Jesus died as our substitute to pay the penalty we owed to God for our sins.

Atonement Terms and Theories

Instead, we have the consensus that humans live in a world where sin exists. The agreement among Christian theologians is that we cannot save ourselves, and we need Jesus to save us. This concept of salvation is a crux in the Christian worldview as Christians affirm Jesus himself saying there is no other way to be saved except through him.[6] Thinking across all denominations, Christians agree that the need for Jesus to save us points to first the gravity of sin, second the greatness of God's love, and third the assurance of our salvation. Significantly, this doctrine is emphasised in the discipleship model all Christians preach and aspire to as we "take up our cross and follow Jesus"[7] and "lay down our lives"[8] for others. Salvation is central to Christian belief and lifestyle, so we have a responsibility to carefully talk about what exactly Jesus did to save us.

Knowing that our salvation is worked through Jesus' death and resurrection, theologians through the past two millennia have theorised based on careful study of the Scriptures how the *atonement* is actually, functionally possible. Atonement is a significant term sometimes used flippantly among Christians to refer to the act of reconciliation between God and humans. Within this, Christians recognise that there was a *sacrifice* which enabled *propitiation* of sins through *substitution* allowing for victory over sin and ultimate *reconciliation* between God and people. Using all these terms in daily conversation is obviously not necessary, but so many people hear them tossed around in Christian contexts without a clear understanding of their meaning. My students are often curious about words that only show up in their Bibles and sermons, so that's why it's worth introducing and defining them here.

The word *atonement* in a general context is about making right something that's been broken; in Christianity, this is specifically about the broken relationship between God and people that only Jesus can fix. The sacrifice concept in Christian theology is linked to the Jewish practice of an animal offering providing a covering or payment for sins committed by a person. A sacrifice is an offering given to make right something that had been wrong. *Propitiation* is just the fancy word for appeasing or atonement; some Bible translations still use this word which is falling out of common speech today.[9] There's nothing wrong with replacing "propitiation" with "sacrifice" in your thinking; you can understand with confidence what the older theologians you might read are referring to. In Christian context, the word *substitution* is important because it refers to how Jesus was our substitute when dying on the cross. The word *redeemer* will be used to describe Jesus in some circles with specific connection to the Hebrew text. Similarly, the word *reconciliation* has special connotation in theological conversations because it generally talks about how Jesus was able to restore the right relationship between God and people.

Broadly speaking, there are six major theories of what happened when Jesus died that makes reconciliation possible. Well known church leaders like Origen and Irenaeus were proponents of a theory called *Christus Victor* which likened Jesus' death and resurrection to a battle against Satan where Jesus Christ was victorious over the great enemy Satan. Around the twelfth century, two other theories emerged. First, Anselm most notably supported and developed the *Satisfaction* theory which proposed our relationship to God was like that of a serf to a feudal lord whom we owed a debt we could not repay. Contemporarily close to Anselm, Peter Abelard is the theologian best known for promoting the *Moral Influence* theory which focused energy on explaining God's great love for us and the lengths to which God would go to restore relationship rather than emphasising our marred sin nature that kept God from us. Laelius Socinus developed what is known as *Socinian* theory which similarly turned more attention to God's love than humanity's sin; his theory proposed that God did not need to forgive but wanted to provide a perfect example for humanity to follow. Many Christian mystics like Meister Eckhart and Theresa of Avila were proponents of *Mystical* theory of atonement that acknowledged our inability to fully understand the divine work of the atonement with our human minds. To some extent, all Christians will acknowledge our inability to perfectly articulate the full details and extent of the atonement. Due to the centrality of salvation in the Christian worldview, theologians have spent a lot of time and effort providing as much clarity as possible from their careful reading of Scriptures.

The most well known theory of atonement in modern western Christianity is the *Governmental* or more specifically, *Penal Substitutionary Atonement* theory. Early church leaders like Cyril and Athanasius held to the governmental kind of theory that God was a righteous judge that needed payment for the sin that separated humanity from such a holy deity. Penal substitutionary atonement theory gives more specific emphasis on how Jesus was our substitute who paid the penalty for our sins because God as a righteous judge needed payment. Some theologians are frustrated with the *penal* or *penalty* element of this substitution theory and focus on how Jesus was a substitute but not to appease an angry, judgy God. N. T. Wright advocates for the combination of the *Christus Victor* perspective with the substitution elements of this other theory. Significantly, we see modern theologians recognizing there is a great deal of mystery at work in the atonement, and like our analogies for the Trinity, there are valuable elements of each perspective to show us things about the work of Jesus while each theory holds limits as well. Each theory is just that - a theory - meant to help us make sense of this great mystery of Jesus reconciling people to God.

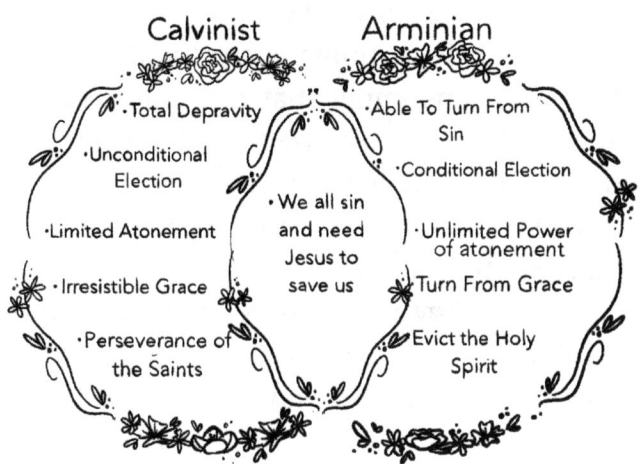

Calvinism and Arminianism

Before ending our look at atonement theories, however, there are two perspectives that need extra attention due to their frequent occurrence in modern western theology. An outgrowth of the focus of God as a righteous judge gained much more traction in the European church during the time of the Reformation. Church leaders like John Calvin and his later critic Joseph Arminius developed their theories about the specific details of how the atonement works under this umbrella of God being a wronged judge demanding penalty against the sin humanity has committed. The focus of Calvin's ideas and those who follow in his tradition was to honour the sovereignty of God in the matter of salvation. Joseph Arminius began as a student of Calvin, but it was the eclipse of the human free will that ultimately led him to criticise and develop a theological response to Calvinism. Significantly, though, both theologians fell comfortably in the governmental theory of atonement as they developed their ideas. Proponents today of a Calvinistic viewpoint hold to several or all "five points" of Calvinism, remembered best in the acronym TULIP.

First, Calvinists believe humans are *totally depraved*. This does not by any means imply that everything humans do is evil but rather that we are so marred by what sin we have committed and that we are inclined to sin rather than to pursue a right relationship with God. Arminians grant that all humans inevitably sin which separates them from a right relationship with God, however, they put considerably more emphasis on the individual's ability to recognise and turn from their sin.

The second major point of Calvinism is the *unconditional election* Calvin recognised as a given throughout the epistles; there is nothing that you have done to deserve your selection by God for salvation. Arminians again emphasise the free will God has given humans as the condition of our election. For the Calvinist, God chose you, so you chose God; for the Arminian, you chose God, so God chose you. Many surface critics of Calvin balk at the notion of election because they conclude that Calvin says if God chooses who to save then he must also choose others for eternal damnation. Some theologians were content with that understanding while Calvin himself was inconsistent in his descriptions.

The third point of Calvinism is *limited atonement* which looks at the actual work of Jesus' death and says it only makes the elect right with God. Therefore, the blood of Jesus is limited in who it atones for in practice though not in power. This nuance matters as Arminians want to emphasise the unlimited power of Jesus' death that could make all people right though some reject the restoration of relationship with God.

Calvinist's fourth point is related to the *irresistible grace* offered to the elect. They propose that if you are offered salvation, there is no way you could turn it down; this in one way focuses on how God would only offer salvation to those who would choose it anyways while also carrying the implication that salvation is too wonderful to deny if you truly understood what was being offered. Still focused on the God-given free will, Arminians reject the idea of irresistible grace in favour of the belief that humans can freely turn down salvation.

The final point of Calvinism is *perseverance of the saints* or sometimes called permanence of salvation. This is the "once saved, always saved" doctrine that proposes you cannot lose your salvation. Adherents to this point would claim that those who turn away from living as Christians were never really saved to begin with. Because we never know where someone's story will end, Calvinists are confident that they can never determine another person's eternal salvation though their words and actions weigh into whether they are considered active in the church community. The Calvinist theologian would say the eternal destination was never altered while the person made choices for or against Jesus in life; alternatively, the Arminian may tend to argue for very real changes in their eternal status correlating to each choice made in their mortal life.

Modern critics of penal substitutionary atonement theory like Brad Jersak and Brian Zahnd argue that these models developed by thinkers in line with Calvin or Arminius, which are focused on God demanding justice, completely miss the biblical narrative that shows God consistently pursuing humanity and working to restore a right relationship with people. What all these theologians agreed on was that the inevitable sins people commit ruin their relationship with God, only Jesus can restore that relationship, and salvation is freely given to whoever wants it. The almost limitless nuances beyond that are attempts to clarify well to converts and Christian disciples how we are able to restore our relationship with God. Their ultimate goal is for all learners to grow in that actual relationship rather than to get lost in the weeds of doctrinal arguments. The consensus of salvation as a free gift matters most as that grace given not earned is what sets Christianity apart from all other major religions. In order to obtain salvation or the best afterlife in other major religions, followers must work to earn this placement or reward; Christianity works the other direction as followers are saved by grace through faith and subsequently live a transformed life of good works out of gratitude to Christ rather than an attempt to earn or maintain salvation.

[1] Lisa Sharon Harper. *The Very Good Gospel* (WaterBrook: Colorado Springs, CO, 2020) 201.

[2] Kevin DeYoung, *The Good News We Almost Forgot* (Moody Publishers: Chicago, IL, 2010) 30.

[3] "Augustine believed that from conception and birth we lack the image of God until it is restored in the sacrament of baptism, and that conception involves us in the sinfulness of nature, sexual intercourse being associated with lustful desire." J. Philip Newell, *Listening for the Heartbeat of God* (Paulist Press: 1997), 14.

[4] Paul E. Little, *Know What You Believe* (InterVarsity Press: Downers Grove, IL, 2008), 102.

[5] R. A. Finlayson, *Reformed Theological Writings* (Mentor: Ross-shire, UK, 1996), 40.

[6] John 14:6, Acts 4:12

[7] Matthew 16:24

[8] John 15:13

[9] For example, Romans 3:25 in the KJV, ESV, and NASB all use "propitiation" whereas the NIV, NLT, and CSB use some combination of "sacrifice" and "atonement" for the same Greek word.

SEVEN

End Times Eschatology

---

the resurrection of the body and life everlasting.

The popular TV show *The Good Place* spent four seasons in a thought experiment about what happens to people when they die. The conclusion was that if we all earned a spot in the good place for doing more good than bad, we would eventually get bored and wouldn't want to spend eternity there. The solution (spoilers) was to request an end - a position akin to what some call annihilation. If whatever comes after death is just limitless torture or limitless pleasure without end, either one sounds unappealing to the masses. Fortunately, that's not what the Bible describes, and it's not what the Christian faith proposes. The end of life as we know it - both in the collective human experience and the individual lives along the way - is a big unknown in Christian theology. There are, as Anglican theologian Tom Wright puts it, signposts that direct us to an idea, but we lack a clear photograph or exact image of what comes at the end or eschaton. *Eschatology* is the fancy word for end times, but it has a more fleshed out definition when theologians use it. Tom Wright explains,

It refers to the strongly held belief of most first-century Jews, and virtually all early Christians, that history was going somewhere under the guidance of God and that where it was going was towards God's new world of justice, healing and hope. The transition from the present world to the new one would be a matter not of the destruction of the present space-time universe, but of its radical healing.[1]

Looking deeper at the Christian views on the end times and the new world after, we'll have to tread carefully around some deeply entrenched imagery that comes not from the Bible but popularised medieval and Renaissance imagination. Christians disagree perhaps most widely on what the end times and afterlife will look like in practicality, but before digging into these differences, let's get straight to the most important point of agreement: all main Christian traditions affirm that Jesus is coming back.

The New Testament writings speak of Jesus' imminent return and Jesus himself as recorded in the Gospels said he was coming back "soon."[2] Because two millennia have passed so far, some Christians reevaluate what "soon" means in an eschatological or end times context. Bishop Kallistos Ware writes from a distinctly Orthodox perspective of Christian doctrine, but his conclusions about the end of the world cross all denominations: "There are, however, at least three things that we are entitled to affirm without ambiguity: that Christ will come again in glory; that at his coming we shall be raised from the dead and judged; and that 'of his kingdom there shall be no end.'"[3] Going into greater detail, he explains the expectation the church has of an anti-Christ though there is ambiguity on what that looks like. Bishop Ware also affirms a significant belief in a bodily resurrection and eternal kingdom.

Some theologians diverging from a Christian worldview tend to suggest this is a metaphorical resurrection, but a significant tenet of the early church was the expectation of our own bodily resurrection based on the experience and promises of Jesus. In fact, the bodily resurrection is perhaps the central point of Tom Wright's three hundred page dense theological text about orthodox Christian beliefs related to eschatology.

Bodily Resurrection

Resurrection hope is language deeply embedded in liturgical prayer traditions though some modern Christian funerals seem to collapse the imagery of the interim state and the final state the Bible distinguishes between. Bereaved loved ones are often desperate for soothing images, and unfortunately some messages are given of happy imagery that is beyond what we can say with confidence based on biblical passages; sometimes it's even in direct conflict. If you're ever at a funeral where someone says, "Heaven has one more angel," you'd be on theologically solid ground to stand up and shout, "That's heresy!" I would highly recommend holding your tongue, though, and remembering instead that while the Bible only gives a little information on what happens after death, we most certainly do not become angels. Based on a wide reading of the Bible, Christians confidently assert that once we die we enter an interim state before our final bodily resurrection.

We're getting into lots of unknowns and speculations and, as usual, disagreements of interpretation. The resurrection language is consistent, however, as is the fact that our resurrection comes altogether as the church (and a separate resurrection of the "unrighteous dead" seems to come after that[4]). Since there is a future resurrection, Christians believe when you die, you enter an interim state to wait for that final bodily resurrection. You get to be a naked soul waiting around to have a new body.

Here's where loads more misconceptions creep in as common Christian language talks about "going to heaven when you die." In one sense, the human death brings the person into God's presence, but in another, heaven is talked about as a complex here/not here reality that leads some theologians to get huffy about our misconception that we just die and are in the final state. Rather than getting lost down that theological rabbit hole, we can focus on the consistency that when we die, our naked soul waits with God for the resurrection where we'll get a renewed body to live on the renewed earth for eternity.

Future Heaven and Earth

This whole renewed earth idea has yet another host of misconceptions and divergent interpretations to wade through next. Our anchor point in the final state is that there is an eternal bodily resurrection for those who choose a restored relationship with God through Jesus. We don't know what it will look like, but theologians agree it will involve some kind of restored relationship with work and worship. Theologians also agree it's not a you-centred, non-stop pleasure party; the final state is centred around God while people get to participate in life to the fullest with God. Before we get to that resurrection and final state, Christians agree some stuff will happen. They argue widely about what that will look like.

Many American Christians have been disproportionately influenced by end times imagery from popular books like *The Late Great Planet Earth* and the *Left Behind* series which represent a narrow theological perspective called premillennial dispensationalism. The theology behind these books is heavily dependent on a very literal reading of the book of Revelation. Significantly, Eastern Orthodox Christians read Revelation as part of their Bible but deliberately make no doctrinal affirmations or statements based on the highly symbolic apocalyptic text. Catholics and Protestants do, however, use Revelation as a source of doctrine, and the next few pages will look at the wide interpretations of a key passage in that book that fleshes out into three views on the end of the world.

Eschatology	Belief
Premillennial	Jesus will return before the millennium to bind Satan and reign with the righteous for 1000 years before judgment.
Amillennial	The "binding of Satan" was the victorious work on the cross and the 1000 year period is now; the Second Coming will result in resurrection.
Postmillennial	Similar to Amillennial, except believe that the present age is leading up to the millennium, which may or may not be literal.

The Millennium

The passage causing all this debate is the second to last chapter of the book, and in it, John describes a millennium, two resurrections (first the righteous, then the unrighteous), and judgement. In modern western churches, more heavily evangelical, fundamentalist, and American, the premillennial view is often the default. Taking the passage more literally, *premillennial* theology anticipates Jesus coming back to bind Satan, raise the righteous in new bodies to reign with him for a literal 1,000 year period before releasing Satan for a brief period, raising the wicked humans for their judgement along with the wicked spiritual beings who will then be cast into the lake of fire (an image in the literal view) before Jesus then reigns forever in the new heaven and earth with the righteous humans. The sticking point of this theology is that we live in the times before the 1,000 years and expect Jesus to arrive to usher in that literal period.

Two other key terms thrown around in end times conversations are *rapture* and *tribulation* which significantly only come into play heavily in the *premillennial* theology. They are, however, worth understanding as many theologians have strong, differing views yet again on when these events will happen. The term *rapture* refers to the removal of believers from earth during the end times in advance of Jesus' second coming. The creative imagination of modern apocalyptic writers usually leaves clothes behind as Christians disappear from earth in an instant. In reality, the Bible doesn't describe the event in detail, but the theological premise is strongly tied to Paul's reference in 1 Thessalonians 4 to living believers meeting Jesus "in the air" when he returns. In theological context, the word *tribulation* refers to a seven year period of trials and judgment on earth. Piecing together different apocalyptic passages, theologians disagree whether the rapture will happen before, during, or after the tribulation; these viewpoints are respectively called pre-tribulation, mid-tribulation, and post-tribulation.

Belief in this literal 1,000 year reign of Jesus happening right after the return of Christ is not the only accepted position within orthodox theology, however. Theologians holding an *amillennial* perspective instead view this chapter of Revelation as figurative. Within this perspective, the current church age is equivalent to the millennium and will end when Jesus returns. In the imagery of Revelation, they interpret the binding of Satan as the victorious work of Christ on the cross. They still believe Jesus will return, but there is no literal 1,000 year period connected to Jesus coming.

Postmillennial theologians have similar views to amillennial theologians with the added anticipation that the church age is in fact leading up to the millennium which they believe may or may not be literal. They believe the world is on a slow and steady trajectory of getting better and the millennium happens once the whole world is converted to Christianity. Their major difference is the belief that Jesus shows up *after* or *post* millennium. Each of these three millennial positions takes its name based on when they believe Jesus will show up again with relation to the described millennium in Revelation 20.

[1] Tom Wright, *Surprised by Hope* (SPCK: London, UK, 2007), 134.
[2] Matthew 24:44, Revelation 22:7
[3] Kallistos Ware, *The Orthodox Way*. (St Vladimir's Seminary Press: Crestwood, NY, 1995), 134.
[4] Revelation 20:5

EIGHT

The Bible Bibliology

The Apostles Creed serves well as a guide through the major points early Christians considered significant in being a part of the Jesus community. Centuries later, Christians look to the Bible in order to learn more about how God wants us to live. Christians call the Bible God's Word and consider the instructions vital in living out God's best for our lives. At its core, Christians believe the Bible helps us to encounter Jesus. This book is significant in the lives of people who want to follow Jesus, and having a Christian worldview requires people to pause and think about why they obey the instructions and believe the doctrines laid out in this ancient book. Establishing the reliability of the text matters, and that is largely what this chapter does. However, that should not be done at the expense of emphasising the fact that any Christian reading the Bible should be looking for ways to become more like Jesus in the way they live, love God, and love other people.

This textbook deliberately leaves out proof-texting from the Bible to make the points about doctrinal belief, but it's impossible to ignore the significance Scripture has in Christians developing and living out their worldview. In fact, Rachel Held

Evans points out in her early book about how she wanted to read the Bible well in order to live in a more God honouring way, "A recent study found that Americans who read their Bibles regularly are 35 percent more likely to say it is important to 'actively seek social and economic justice' than those who own a Bible but don't bother to open it too often."[1] The Bible and the interpretation of it are fundamental in understanding the broader Christian worldview. However, as in every previous chapter, there are disagreements among Christians related to this topic. Particularly with this subject, disagreements centre on how to interpret the Bible and occasionally even which books should be prioritised. Instead of getting caught up in interpretive theories, this chapter will focus[2] on the selection of texts within the Christian canon and the reliability of the modern texts and translations. The term *canon* refers to the books that are accepted and understood as sacred texts.

The Books and the Original Words

As Christianity continued growing and sharing the message of Jesus, churches carried copies of the Jewish sacred texts to their new gatherings though the rapidly expanding church quickly became more non-Jewish than Jewish in membership, and some leaders were not trained to distinguish between the texts considered sacred in Judaism versus those just revered as quality wisdom meditation literature. This is where we find what Protestants call the *apocryphal* texts that the reformers of the 1500s chose to exclude from the canon. The thirty-nine books considered part of the Christian Old Testament, however, are taken from a long history of Jewish religious leaders who preserved and cared for the copies of the sacred texts. In the Hebrew Bible, the same thirty-nine books Protestants group into four categories are actually divided into just twenty-four books that are ordered in only three sections. These books considered the Old Testament canon by Christians today were considered the complete canon of ancient Hebrew culture as well. Ancient Jewish historian Josephus noted the consensus among Jewish people that their canon had closed in the time of Artaxerxes, so by 424 BCE all of the Hebrew Bible was complete. The texts Catholics include in their Bible as the *deuterocanonical* books (or "second canon")[3] were composed after this date; Protestants refer to those wisdom writings as *apocrypha*.

The preservation of these texts over centuries is unique among ancient writings. Because these were considered holy writings, the ancient Hebrews developed careful maintenance and copying systems to preserve the writings. A particular group of copyists called the Masoretes were particularly known for their attention to detail as they checked each new copy for errors by counting letters and destroying copies found with mistakes. The Masoretic Text is an Aramaic version of the Old Testament that is considered to be the most authoritative version of the collected texts. Textual critics evaluate the veracity of manuscripts based on two primary factors - the quantity and date of manuscripts in question. How many mostly similar copies do we have and how close are these copies in date to the original text? These two questions are of utmost importance, but the quality of the Masoretic texts holds greater credibility. Significantly, the discovery of the Dead Sea Scrolls in 1947 showed 98% similarity from the Great Isaiah Scroll to the existing manuscripts used in modern translations. The Dead Sea Scrolls are significantly older than those other manuscripts scholars have used for translation, validating the preservation of the text through the centuries. Modern translators rely heavily on the Masoretic tradition manuscripts in addition to the famous Greek translation of the Old Testament that would have been familiar to Jesus and his contemporaries. Scholars have long called this text the *Septuagint* because it's traditionally attributed to seventy scholars who translated the original

Hebrew into Greek and the name comes from the Latin word for seventy. When it comes to determining the reliability of the Old Testament manuscripts, the quality of Hebrew scribes makes up for the limited quantity.

Much the opposite is true when determining the reliability of the New Testament text. As the Christian church rapidly expanded across the world from Jerusalem to Judea to the farthest reaches of the Roman Empire, letters from the apostles were copied frequently and distributed widely. When these early Christians were gathering, they were first considering themselves a sect of Judaism and using the Hebrew Bible as sacred text with letters the apostles wrote as authoritative instructions in godly living. Within the first century, there were some letters and instructions that became valued more than others and soon considered inspired. Many different lists of the most important texts circulated in the first couple centuries of the Christian church though, and it wasn't until the Council of Carthage in 397 that there was a formal affirmation of the list of twenty-seven books considered canon today. This, however, was an affirmation of the canon already widely in use. Three significant criteria used to determine inclusion on this list at Carthage were the apostolic authority assigned to the book, the use and recognition of it by the churches already, and the teaching of sound doctrine. The concept of apostolic authority was not that the text was written by one of the twelve apostles but rather that it had been given their stamp of approval by connection to the author. For example, the Gospel of Mark was not written by an apostle but is considered to have apostolic authority from Peter. Similarly, the works written by Luke bear the apostolic authority of Paul based on their close relationship. Christians today believe the books included in their canon are the right books because they were received and used as such by the early Christians.

The manuscript reliability is also completely trustworthy based on any evaluation of textual criticism. For context, the veracity or the content of Homer's Iliad is never doubted among critics based on the number of ancient manuscripts we have. Based on a generous look at the various ancient manuscripts available, scholars would say around 1,800 exist - this includes most which are only small portions rather than complete copies. The smaller number 643 is cited often, but even allowing for a more generous number, the volume pales in comparison to the over 5,000 of original language New Testament manuscripts accounted for. Just as scholars can consider the Septuagint, an ancient translation of the Old Testament, a highly reliable source, there is a wealth of ancient manuscripts of early Christian translations of the New Testament as well. When these are included, there are an additional 18,500 plus manuscripts.[4] Modern archeology is constantly discovering new manuscripts, but the numbers are overwhelmingly in favour of the reliability of the New Testament over any other undisputed ancient text. A further point of reliability is the gap between the discovered manuscripts and estimated dates of composition. There is an estimated 400 years between the copy we have of Homer's Iliad and the date of composition whereas the earliest New Testament manuscript is a mere fifty years from the estimated original writing. Criticism of the text of the Christian Bible being unreliable because it is so far removed from the original authors is simply not viable; there is too much evidence to disprove that false claim.

Translation

When the printing press was invented in 1453, the Latin Vulgate translation of the Bible was the first printed book. From then on, the number of copies of the Bible increased exponentially. Today hundreds of translations exist in English alone, and Wycliffe Bible Translators estimate at the time of this publication that nearly 700 languages have a complete Bible translated and over 1,500 have a complete New Testament. There are also over 2,600 ongoing Bible translation projects globally. Bible translators have a wealth of texts to work with to reliably discover what was originally written. However, there are several considerations for translators as they work to accurately transfer content from the original language to the target language. The largest tension is between the literal translation and the idiomatic translation. Literal, also called formal translation, philosophy emphasises the very words as significant and needing functional equivalence in the target language. This often places more value on the *verbal* inspiration of Scripture, believing these very words were carefully chosen by God and delivered to each biblical author. Idiomatic translation philosophy considers the broader thoughts biblical authors were communicating through metaphors and other sorts of figurative language. This other theory gives more weight to the *plenary* inspiration of Scripture, believing the thoughts and ideas are what are most significant, and each biblical author used the figurative language and cultural reference points that would most effectively communicate to their original audience. Subsequently, more idiomatic translations have more thought for thought translation while formal translations work to preserve the words with less idioms translated to the target language.

Bible translators are constantly working to navigate the extremes of these theories to deliver the message from the original writer to the modern audience both faithfully and effectively. Greatest among the struggles is that languages are living things and constantly adapting. Each year dictionaries must adjust how words are used colloquially and add new terms common in culture. The original translation team of the King James Bible recognised this very issue and included in their preface their edition granting that their goal was to make a readable version of the Bible to contemporary English speakers but that it would eventually need to be updated and redone as the English language changed over time. This note is no longer included in modern editions of the King James Bible, nor is it read or known to those who adhere to the "King James only" perspective on biblical literacy.

Readers can comfortably trust the text of the Bible and the translations published today. As mentioned at the start of this chapter, though, the most significant detail about the Bible is that it is God's words given to people to help us live and love well. None of the facts about text and translation matter if we don't bother reading the Bible or if we read it and make sloppy interpretations. The Bible is meant to change us as we read it, to help us love God and others better.

Unfortunately, there are a lot of details about the text that are taken for granted, misquoted, or misrepresented. Biblical literacy is a privilege often wasted in the Western world. As this textbook is an overview of Christian doctrine, the goal is to show how different Christians have used this same Bible to affirm a small core of unified beliefs while also seeing many tensions and disagreements on how to best understand and live according to other passages. Rather than providing a narrow interpretive lens, this hopefully stands as an encouragement to engage the biblical text itself respectfully with humility and an open mind to see how so many people have dedicated their lives to the God it claims to represent. As Levar Burton famously taught a generation about reading, "You don't have to take my word for it."

[1] Rachel Held Evans, *A Year of Biblical Womanhood* (Thomas Nelson: Nashville, TN, 2012), 228.

[2] While the purpose of this present book covers the textual issues of the Bible, it's too important to ignore that the Bible as a whole is not a dry textbook for Christians; the purpose of reading the Bible, as Ray Lubeck says in *Read the Bible for a Change*, is to foster loving relationships with God and other people.

[3] "Deutero" means "second" which is why we name the fifth book of the Bible Deuteronomy since it is the second telling of the law.

[4] These numbers come from "The Bibliographical Test" article that Drs. Josh McDowell and Clay Jones updated online in 2014.

Selected Bibliography

Boyd, Gregory A. *Is God to Blame?: Beyond Pat Answers to the Problem of Suffering*. Downers Grove, IL: IV Press, 2003.

Challies, Tim, and Josh Byers. *Visual Theology: Seeing and Understanding the Truth About God*. Grand Rapids, MI: Zondervan, 2016.

Crossan, John Dominic. *How to Read the Bible and Still Be a Christian: Struggling with Divine Violence from Genesis through Revelation*. San Francisco, CA: Harper One, 2016.

Deverell, Garry Worete. *Gondwana Theology: A Trawloolway Man Reflects on Christian Faith*. Eugene, OR: Wipf & Stock, 2018.

DeYoung, Kevin. *The Good News We Almost Forgot: Rediscovering the Gospel in a 16th Century Catechism*. Chicago, IL: Moody Publishers, 2010.

Evans, Rachel Held. *A Year of Biblical Womanhood: How a Liberated Woman Found Herself Sitting on Her Roof, Covering Her Head, and Calling Her Husband "Master."* Nashville, TN: Thomas Nelson, 2012.

Finlayson, R. A. *Reformed Theological Writings*. Ross-shire, UK: Mentor, 1996.

Gay, Jerome. "All White Everything." Essay. In *Urban Apologetics: Restoring Black Dignity with the Gospel*, edited by Eric Mason, 13–25. Grand Rapids, MI: Zondervan Reflective, 2021.

Harper, Lisa Sharon. *The Very Good Gospel: How Everything Wrong Can Be Made Right*. Colorado Springs, CO: WaterBrook, 2020.

Little, Paul E. *Know What You Believe*. Downers Grove, IL: IVP Books, 2008.

Lubeck, Ray. *Read the Bible for a Change*. Wipf & Stock, 2010.

Mason, Eric. "Engaging Hebrew Israelites." Essay. In *Urban Apologetics: Restoring Black Dignity with the Gospel*, edited by Eric Mason, 92-114. Grand Rapids, MI: Zondervan Reflective, 2021.

McDowell, Josh D, and Clay Jones. "The Bibliographical Test." Josh McDowell. CRU, August 13, 2014. https://www.josh.org/wp-content/uploads/Bibliographical-Test-Update-08.13.14.pdf.

McGrath, Alister E. *Historical Theology: Introduction to the History of Christian Thought*. Oxford, UK: Blackwell, 1998.

Merritt, Jonathan. *Learning to Speak God from Scratch: Why Sacred Words Are Vanishing -- and How We Can Revive Them*. New York, NY: Convergent, 2018.

Newell, J. Philip. *Listening for the Heartbeat of God: A Celtic Spirituality*. Mahwah, NJ: Paulist Press, 1997.

Polkinghorne, John C. *Quantum Physics and Theology: An Unexpected Kinship*. New Haven: Yale University Press, 2007.

Swoboda, A. J. *Messy: God Likes It That Way*. Grand Rapids, MI: Kregel Publications, 2012.

Tait, Stephanie. "A Liturgy of Disability." Essay. In *A Rhythm of Prayer: A Collection of Meditations for Renewal*, edited by Sarah Bessey, 78-83. Colorado Springs, CO: Convergent Books, 2021.

van Deusen Hungsinger, Deborah. *Pray Without Ceasing: Revitalizing Pastoral Care*. Grand Rapids, MI: William B. Eerdmans Publishing, 2006.

Ware, Kallistos. *The Orthodox Way*. Crestwood, NY: St Vladimir's Seminary Press, 1995.

Wright, Tom. *Surprised by Hope*. London, UK: SPCK, 2007.

Acknowledgements

Eric Gibson first suggested I write my own textbook for my course after listening to my frustration with the shortcomings of the one I'd been teaching. Many thanks for your confidence in my learning and ability, your encouragement and support in the endeavour, and for being such a valuable coworker and friend.

I take full responsibility for any errors in this text, but I also offer my incredible thanks to Mark Wells, Tracy Welterlen, Eric Gibson, Richard Yancey, Sofia Liberti, Tessa Sydnor, Missy Takano, Carol Bonham, EunJin Kim, Abby McKell, Injin Lee, and Jacob Shuman who offered insights and corrections to initial drafts to help make this version better.

In addition to the quoted texts and ideas from the other sources listed in the selected bibliography, I'm indebted to Dr. Karl Kutz and Dr. Rex Koivisto who taught me years ago; the last two chapters in particular have a lot of information summarised from the notes I kept when taking their classes while I was an undergraduate student at Multnomah University.

Leah Finke, thank you for your incredible graphics. Givorgy Kraskoff, thank you for being a champion of all the other pre-publication formatting details including cover design.

Drew Kelsey, thanks for giving me a reason to plan a second edition before the first one was even in print. This book is not only for my students, but for young people like you thinking carefully about their faith.

A final shout out goes to the students in my fall 2021 semester who voted for the "extra" work of giving feedback while reading this textbook.

This book is meant to be a blessing, so if you are using it as a textbook at an international Christian school, email me at sainthewett@gmail.com for free curriculum to use with it.

www.ingramcontent.com/pod-product-compliance
Lightning Source LLC
Chambersburg PA
CBHW051843160426
43209CB00006B/1140